EXPRESS MEALS

→

175 DELICIOUS DISHES YOU CAN MAKE IN 30 MINUTES OR LESS

EXPRESS MEALS

175 DELICIOUS DISHES YOU CAN MAKE IN 30 MINUTES OR LESS

LIZ FRANKLIN

DUNCAN BAIRD PUBLISHERS

LONDON

Express Meals
Liz Franklin

First published in the United Kingdom and Ireland
in 2012 by
Duncan Baird Publishers Ltd
Sixth Floor, Castle House
75–76 Wells Street, London W1T 3QH

Conceived, created and designed by
Duncan Baird Publishers

Managing Editor: Grace Cheetham
Editor: Nicola Graimes
Managing Designer: Manisha Patel
Designer: Gail Jones
Commissioned Photography: Toby Scott
Food Stylist: Kate Blinman
Prop Stylist: Clare Hunt

British Library Cataloguing-in-Publication Data:
A CIP record for this book is available from the
British Library

ISBN: 978-1-84899-025-8

10 9 8 7 6 5 4 3 2 1

Typeset in Rockwell
Colour reproduction by XY Digital
Printed in Singapore by Imago

Publisher's note
While every care has been taken in compiling the recipes for this
book, Duncan Baird Publishers, or any other persons who have been
involved in working on this publication, cannot accept responsibility
for any errors or omissions, inadvertent or not, that may be found in the
recipes or text, nor for any problems that may arise as a result of
preparing one of these recipes or following the advice contained in
this work. If you are pregnant or breastfeeding or have any special
dietary requirements or medical conditions, it is important to consult a
medical professional before following any of the recipes in this book.
Ill or elderly people, babies, young children and women who are
pregnant or breastfeeding should avoid any recipes containing lightly
cooked eggs.

Acknowledgements
With huge thanks to Grace Cheetham, Nicola Graimes and the team at
DBP for helping to turn Express Meals into such a beautiful book – and
to Toby Scott, Kate Blinman and Clare Hunt for the beautiful
photography. Also, masses of love and thanks to my wonderful parents
and my three sons, Chris, Oli and Tim, for their love, support and
encouragement in everything I do.

Notes on the recipes
Unless otherwise stated:
All recipes serve 4
Use medium fruit, vegetables and eggs
Use fresh ingredients, including herbs
Do not mix metric and imperial measurements:
1 tsp = 5ml; 1 tbsp = 15ml; 1 cup = 250ml

CONTENTS

INTRODUCTION

For most of us, time is something we never seem to have enough of. We're so wrapped up in the hustle and bustle of our busy lives that cooking often becomes an afterthought – it's tempting just to grab a takeaway or buy something to pop in the microwave. But producing a quick, nutritious meal needn't take an age or be complicated, and it can certainly be enjoyable... fast food can be fun food!

The collection of recipes in *Express Meals* shows how you can create a meal from scratch using fresh ingredients in anything from five to thirty minutes. It really is possible to cook up something sensational in the time it would take to pick up a takeaway, or heat a ready-meal; and it's not only doable but also rewarding.

There is so much to gain from getting into the kitchen and rustling up anything from a simple dinner to a fantastic feast for friends. Sitting down together – eating, chatting, listening, laughing and catching up with friends and family – is precious. The stresses and strains of a hurried day can seem halved, or the excitement of good news doubled, when we sit down to share a great meal in good company.

ABOUT THE RECIPES

One of the most important features of this book is that the recipes are "complete" meals, so they contain all the components necessary for a well-balanced dinner. Reassuringly, this means that each recipe features any accompaniments, whether it is pasta, rice, potatoes, pulses or simply crusty bread, as well as side dishes such as vegetables or salad. What's more, each recipe can be made from start to table within the time contraints – whether it is five minutes or thirty minutes.

Inspired by the cuisines of the world, there should be a recipe in this book to whet your appetite. A wide variety of ingredients is more readily available than ever before, so it's possible to create my recipes for a fragrant Spiced Salmon in Noodle Miso Broth, Mexican Chilli Beans with Avocado Cream or Baked Chicken Breasts in Tomato & Mascarpone, for example, with ease and in next to no time. Additionally, taking charge of what you eat enables you to ensure meals are fresh, nutritious and not loaded with salt, sugar and any unwanted additives.

The more we realize just how much enjoyment, satisfaction and fantastic food can come out of spending even a short amount of time in the kitchen, the more enthusiastic and confident we are likely to become about cooking. So, I've put together lots of fabulous, fuss-free recipes that are made from simple, easily accessible ingredients, whether you're looking to make a speedy after-work meal, or something a little more special.

There are no long-simmered stocks, complicated sauces or mind-bogglingly long lists of ingredients either. When time is at a premium, no one wants to spend hours in the supermarket searching for hard-to-find ingredients. There are substantial salads, mouth-watering meat dishes, delectable fish-feasts and meals for vegetarians that meat-eaters will find hard to resist, too. And I've also added tips that will help to make your time in the kitchen as enjoyable and stress free as possible.

STORECUPBOARD BASICS

For the cook in a hurry, a well-stocked storecupboard becomes a real treasure trove. Fill it with ingredients that you use on a regular basis in order to make life easier and meals more varied. Now's the time to clear out those half-empty packets of something bought many years ago; spices that are so past their use-by-date that their flavour is long gone; or jars of powders and pastes purchased for one-off recipes that now look decidedly unpalatable.

Ideally, treat the storecupboard as a significant part of your kitchen – make it a stash of indispensable basics that you can build upon. So if it looks like something from *The Land That Time Forgot*, give it a good clear out and start over!

Stock your storecupboard with handy basics that will enable you to produce the kind of meals you love to eat, time and time again. Staples such as tinned tomatoes, tinned pulses, pasta, rice, lentils, quick-cook grains, noodles, jars of passata, punchy pastes for curries, a small selection of everyday spices, and, it goes without saying, those essential seasonings, salt and pepper, are all a must.

Always have extra virgin olive oil to hand – ideally a blended one for cooking, and something a little more special for drizzling over meat, fish or vegetables, as well as dressing salads, and even to serve as a dip with vegetables and bread as an easy, pre-dinner appetizer.

A bottle each of balsamic, red and white wine vinegar will always come in handy, and jars of olives, roasted red peppers, artichoke hearts, capers and anchovies are brilliant for adding a little oomph to all manner of dishes.

For Asian-style suppers, key ingredients such as sesame oil and soy, fish and sweet chilli sauces are also indispensible.

So, with a little organization and planning, you now have the basics to whip up quick and tasty meals.

SHREWD SHOPPING

A hectic lifestyle means that most of us need to shop in the most time-effective and expedient way. For many of us that means large stores and supermarkets, but it's not always possible to fit in a mad trolley dash in the middle of a busy day, and how many of us want to factor in a frenetic shop at the end of a long day at work?

Shopping online may save time and is certainly useful for bulk or long-lasting items, but it is easy to switch onto auto-pilot and become very repetitive in our shopping habits. Choosing fresh fruit, vegetables, meat or fish is better done in person, and sometimes it may be quicker to pop into a local butcher, greengrocer or fishmonger, if you're lucky enough to have them. It's also good to support the local guy on the street,

or perhaps consider a box-delivery scheme for fresh fruit and vegetables. And even the busiest of us might make time to sow a few seeds in a pot to give a supply of fresh herbs on the kitchen windowsill – it doesn't take as long as you think, is economical and fun!

In a move to eat well in less time, it's a good idea to try and stay in tune with the seasons when buying fresh fruit and vegetables. That way, you can also keep costs down and ensure that meals are as nutritious and tasty as possible. What's more, when buying loose fresh produce you negate the need for unnecessary packaging. It's also worth considering that pre-packaged convenience foods often contain unwanted additives, many of which have been linked to health problems. By buying good-quality ingredients and preparing fresh food yourself, you have much more control over these vital considerations – and mealtimes become special again, rather than being a rushed affair simply for the purpose of re-fuelling.

For the time-pressured cook, it makes absolute sense to get the best from your supplier, wherever you choose to shop. When you're buying fish fillets, for example, whether from a high street fishmonger or over the counter at the supermarket, make sure they are filleted, if necessary, as well as gutted, pin-boned and scaled.

Ask the butcher to trim meat and remove unnecessary fat and bones, if required. Any supplier worth their salt will be pleased to offer a good service.

BE ADAPTABLE

Don't be afraid to substitute ingredients when following the recipes in this book. If you can't get exactly what is specified in the recipe, or you want to ring the changes by using a favourite ingredient, consider the characteristics of the dish and the cooking method, rather than following it in every detail. That way, you can adjust and adapt the recipe to suit your preferences.

If the recipe suggests an accompaniment, don't feel you need to be precise, especially with simple things such as bread, salad leaves or vegetables. They are only suggestions and it's best to follow your own personal preferences and what you have to hand. Think about ingredients that make good bed-fellows in terms of texture and flavour – although you must remember to factor in the cooking times too. There's no point planning to do roast potatoes alongside a recipe from the 10-minute chapter. The more you cook, the more expert your palate and kitchen skills will become, and the more your intuition will guide you.

BE PREPARED

For those of you who are fairly new to cooking, some of the recipes may take a little longer at the start, but relax, enjoy and have confidence in your ability to make great, tasty meals – and you're sure to become speedier soon!

For all levels of ability, it goes without saying that the buzzword for the busy cook is undoubtedly "be prepared" (okay, well two words). A major cause of delay (and frustration) when cooking is finding that you're mid-way through preparing a dish, and you haven't got everything you need. Scrabbling around the cupboards or rummaging through the fridge to look for a vital ingredient, only to find subsequently that you haven't got it, is something we probably all do at some stage, but it really doesn't help create calm and harmony in the kitchen.

Plan meals ahead, decide what you are going to cook, read through the whole recipe before you start, and get all the ingredients and tools you need to hand. To be organized is to be halfway there.

So, all that remains to be said is that I hope you enjoy cooking and eating your way through the recipes that follow as much as I did developing and writing them. You'll soon discover that less time doesn't mean less tempting – or less tasty!

FIVE MINUTES DOESN'T SOUND MUCH TIME TO PREPARE AND COOK A MEAL, BUT IT REALLY CAN BE DONE! USING TEMPTING TIME SAVERS, SUCH AS SMOKED FISH, SPECIFIC CUTS OF MEAT AND FRESH PASTA, IT'S POSSIBLE TO CREATE A RANGE OF MOUTH-WATERING MEALS, INCLUDING MINUTE STEAKS WITH BLUE CHEESE SAUCE AND SMOKED SALMON TAGLIATELLE.

SMOKED CHICKEN, AVOCADO & WALNUT SALAD

Smoked chicken adds a deliciously different touch to this salad, but you could use cold roast chicken as an alternative.

4 cooked smoked chicken breasts, skinned, boned and shredded • 4 large handfuls of rocket leaves • 2 ripe avocados, pitted and sliced • 2 handfuls of walnut halves

DRESSING: 6 tbsp extra virgin olive oil • 2 tbsp red wine vinegar • 1 tsp wholegrain mustard • a pinch of sugar • salt and freshly ground black pepper

TO SERVE: crusty bread

1 Put the chicken in a large salad bowl. Add the rocket leaves and avocado, then scatter the walnuts over the top.

2 Put all the ingredients for the dressing into a screw-topped jar, season with a little salt and pepper, then shake well until the dressing emulsifies. Pour enough of the dressing over the salad to lightly coat it, then toss well. Serve with slices of crusty bread.

CHICKEN NOODLE SOUP

Thai tom yum paste, which can be found in good supermarkets and oriental food shops, makes a useful and versatile flavouring for soups and other Thai dishes. Adjust the amount to suit your personal preference, starting with just a teaspoonful of paste and then adding more to taste, so that you don't end up overdoing it.

1.5 litres/52fl oz/6 cups chicken stock • 1–2 tsp tom yum paste, or to taste • 200g/7oz cooked skinless, boneless chicken breast strips • 300g/10½oz straight-to-wok Singapore noodles • 200g/7oz sugar snap peas • 6 spring onions, chopped

1 Pour the chicken stock into a large saucepan and stir in the tom yum paste. Bring to the boil, then turn the heat down and add the chicken and noodles. Simmer the soup for 2 minutes, stirring from time to time to separate the noodles.
2 Add the sugar snap peas and spring onions to the pan, then cook for 1 minute before serving.

SPINACH, PROSCIUTTO & EGG SALAD

The saltiness of crisp prosciutto marries beautifully with spinach and sun-dried tomatoes – and a runny fried egg on top makes one of those amazingly quick but comforting meals. Buy the sun-dried tomatoes in oil from the deli section of your supermarket or a good delicatessen.

3 tbsp olive oil • 4 large eggs • 8 slices prosciutto • 4 large handfuls of baby spinach leaves • 300g/10½oz bottled mixed wild mushrooms in olive oil, drained • 8 sun-dried or sun-blush tomatoes in olive oil, drained and coarsely chopped • 1–2 tsp balsamic vinegar • salt and freshly ground black pepper

TO SERVE: baguette

1 Heat the olive oil in a large, non-stick frying pan over a medium heat. Fry the eggs for 3–4 minutes until the white is set but the yolk remains runny.
2 In the meantime, heat a separate non-stick frying pan or griddle pan over a high heat. Dry-fry the prosciutto for 1–2 minutes, turning once, until crisp and golden.
3 At the same time, put the spinach in a large salad bowl. Add the mushrooms, sun-dried tomatoes and balsamic vinegar. Season with salt and pepper, then toss well until combined.
4 Top each serving of salad with a fried egg and the prosciutto, and acompany with slices of baguette.

PROSCIUTTO, PECORINO & GREEN LEAF SALAD

Salty prosciutto and crumbly pecorino combine beautifully with sweet, tangy balsamic vinegar and peppery salad leaves. Use your favourite prosciutto in this recipe – Parma ham, Speck or San Danielle all work well.

4 large handfuls of mixed salad leaves (including spinach, rocket and watercress, if possible) • 12 slices of prosciutto, torn into pieces • 125g/4½oz aged pecorino cheese
DRESSING: 6 tbsp extra virgin olive oil • 2 tbsp balsamic vinegar • salt and freshly ground black pepper

TO SERVE: breadsticks

1 Put the salad leaves in a serving bowl and top with the prosciutto. Using a vegetable peeler, slice the pecorino into shavings and add to the bowl.
2 To make the dressing, whisk the olive oil and balsamic vinegar together and season with salt and pepper.
3 Add enough of the dressing to lightly coat the leaves and toss everything well. Serve the salad with breadsticks on the side.

HOT MORTADELLA PANINI

These panini are best served warm so the fat from the mortadella melts into the bread, making it moist and tasty. Fans of spicy food will love a drizzle of chilli oil, too.

4 small ciabatta, cut in half • 8 slices of mortadella •150g/5½oz roasted peppers in olive oil, drained and sliced • 1 small bunch of watercress • lemon juice or chilli oil, to drizzle (optional)

TO SERVE: Italian-style mixed leaf salad

1 Preheat the grill to high.
2 Grill the ciabatta, crust-side up, for 1–2 minutes until lightly toasted. Turn the bread over and toast for another 1 minute.
3 Top one half of each ciabatta with the mortadella, roasted peppers and watercress, then squeeze over a little lemon juice or drizzle with chilli oil, if using. Place the other half of ciabatta on top and serve with an Italian-style mixed leaf salad.

GRILLED SALAMI PITTA PIZZAS

These pizzas make a great speedy and satisfying impromptu meal.

6 tbsp good-quality tomato passata or tomato sauce • ½ tsp dried oregano • 4 round pitta breads • 200g/7oz mozzarella cheese, drained and torn into pieces • 12 slices of salami • 1 tbsp extra virgin olive oil • a few baby chard leaves • salt and freshly ground black pepper

TO SERVE: mixed leaf salad

1 Preheat the grill to very high.
2 In the meantime, mix the passata with the oregano. Spoon the sauce on top of the pitta breads and spread out evenly, leaving a border. Top with the salami and mozzarella, then season with salt and pepper.
3 Drizzle a little olive oil over each pizza and grill for 2 minutes until the cheese is bubbling and melted. Scatter the baby chard leaves over the top and serve straightaway with a mixed leaf salad.

BRESAOLA & ARTICHOKE SALAD

Bresaola is an Italian speciality made from lean beef cured in a very particular way, producing a gorgeous meat that is very low in fat. Speck or Parma ham would also work well as alternatives.

16 slices of bresaola • 350g/12oz bottled artichoke hearts in olive oil, drained • 100g/3½oz Parmesan cheese • 1 lemon, cut into thin wedges • 2 tbsp extra virgin olive oil • 1 tbsp chopped parsley leaves (optional) • freshly ground black pepper

TO SERVE: sun-dried tomato and olive focaccia bread

1 Arrange the bresaola on a serving platter and top with the artichoke hearts. Using a vegetable peeler, slice the Parmesan into shavings and scatter over the top.
2 Squeeze the juice from 1–2 lemon wedges over, to taste. Arrange the remaining lemon wedges around the platter. Drizzle with the olive oil and season with pepper. Sprinkle with parsley, if using, before serving with slices of focaccia.

MINUTE STEAKS WITH BLUE CHEESE SAUCE >

This rich and creamy blue cheese sauce takes next to no time to make and is delicious with tender steak. You could try other types of blue cheese, if preferred.

150g/5½oz Gorgonzola cheese, crumbled • 4 tbsp dry white wine • 3–4 small thyme sprigs • 4 minute steaks • 1 tbsp olive oil • salt and freshly ground black pepper

TO SERVE: watercress salad and walnut bread

1 To make the sauce, put the Gorgonzola, wine and thyme sprigs in a small saucepan. Cook over a medium heat for 2–3 minutes, stirring regularly, until the Gorgonzola has melted and the sauce is smooth and creamy. Season with salt and pepper.
2 In the meantime, heat a griddle pan until very hot. Brush the steaks with the olive oil, season with salt and pepper and griddle for 1 minute on each side.
3 Spoon the sauce over the steaks and serve straightaway with a watercress salad and slices of walnut bread.

TUNA & BEAN SALAD

This works well with tinned tuna in olive oil, but for the best flavour look for the top-quality tuna fillets bottled in extra virgin olive oil.

4 large handfuls of mixed salad leaves • 400g/14oz bottled or tinned tuna fillets in extra virgin olive oil, drained and flaked into chunks • 400g/14oz tinned cannellini beans, drained and rinsed • 1 ripe beefsteak tomato, deseeded and roughly chopped • 1 small onion, chopped • 1 small handful of parsley, leaves chopped • 4 tbsp extra virgin olive oil • juice of ½ lemon, or to taste • salt and freshly ground black pepper

TO SERVE: olive ciabatta bread

1 Put the salad leaves in a serving bowl. Add the tuna, cannellini beans, tomato, onion and parsley.
2 Mix together the olive oil and lemon juice, then spoon it over the salad. Season with salt and pepper, then gently toss everything together. Serve with slices of olive ciabatta.

< TUNA CARPACCIO WITH CAPER DRESSING

The colder the tuna, the easier it is to cut into paper-thin slices. Or you could ask your fishmonger to slice the tuna for you.

6 tbsp extra virgin olive oil • 1 handful of salted capers, rinsed and drained • 300g/10½oz very cold, sushi-grade whole tuna loin, cut into very thin slices • juice of ½ lemon • 4 handfuls of rocket leaves

TO SERVE: lemon wedges and wholegrain bread

1 Heat 2 tablespoons of the olive oil in a small, non-stick frying pan until very hot. Add the capers and fry for about 30 seconds until puffed up. Remove the capers from the pan and drain on kitchen paper.
2 In the meantime, arrange the sliced tuna on four serving plates.
3 Put the capers into a bowl and stir in the remaining olive oil and lemon juice until combined. Spoon the dressing over the tuna.
4 Top each serving with a handful of rocket leaves and a lemon wedge. Serve with slices of bread.

SMOKED SALMON TAGLIATELLE

This makes an elegant dinner, and its short preparation and cooking time leaves lots of time for you to spend with your guests.

500g/1lb 2oz fresh egg tagliatelle • 100ml/3½fl oz/ generous ⅓ cup double cream • finely grated zest of 1 lemon • 1 tbsp snipped chives • 250g/9oz smoked salmon pieces • salt and freshly ground black pepper

TO SERVE: baby spinach leaf salad

1 Bring a large saucepan of salted water to the boil and cook the tagliatelle for 2 minutes or until al dente.
2 In the meantime, gently heat the double cream, lemon zest and chives in a large saucepan for 1 minute or until warmed through. Season with salt and pepper.
3 Using pasta tongs, lift the cooked pasta from the pan and add to the warm cream mixture. Add the salmon and turn until combined. Serve straightaway with a baby spinach leaf salad.

SMOKED TROUT, SUGAR SNAP & AVOCADO SALAD

Packed with flavour and bursting with vitamins and beneficial fats, this salad makes a super-healthy and quickly prepared dinner.

8 cooked smoked trout fillets, skin removed and flaked into large chunks • 2 handfuls of sugar snap peas • 2 ripe avocados, pitted and thinly sliced • juice of 1 lime • 4 tbsp avocado oil • freshly ground black pepper

TO SERVE: seeded bread

1 Put the trout, sugar snap peas and avocado in a serving bowl.
2 Add the lime juice and drizzle the avocado oil over. Season with pepper and gently turn until combined. Serve the salad with slices of seeded bread.

SEARED SCALLOP & PEA SHOOT SALAD

Choose fresh king scallops from a reliable fishmonger for this vibrant salad – frozen scallops may be plumped up with water and tend to shrink when cooked.

4 tbsp extra virgin olive oil • 12 fresh king scallops • ½ tsp ginger paste • ½ tsp caster sugar • a pinch of dried chilli flakes • juice of 1 lime • 4 handfuls of pea shoots • 1 handful of mangetout • coarse sea salt

TO SERVE: lime wedges and baguette

1 Heat 1 tablespoon of the olive oil in a griddle pan over a high heat. Season the scallops with a little salt and sear them for 1 minute on each side.
2 Mix together the ginger paste, caster sugar, chilli flakes, lime juice and the remaining olive oil.
3 Place the pea shoots and mangetout in a large bowl then pour the dressing over and toss well. Serve the scallops straightaway with the salad, lime wedges and slices of baguette.

SALT & CHILLI SQUID WITH LIME

Tasty and simple, this recipe makes a great light meal served with a mixed leaf and herb salad. Alternatively, a salad of crisp Asian-style vegetables would also be delicious.

12 medium cleaned and prepared squid, cut into 5cm/2in pieces, and tentacles reserved • 2–3 tbsp olive oil • ½ tsp dried chilli flakes, or to taste • 2 spring onions, finely chopped • juice of 1 lime • 1 tbsp chopped coriander leaves • salt and freshly ground black pepper

TO SERVE: lime wedges, mixed leaf and herb salad and crusty bread

1 Score a diamond pattern lightly across the flesh of the squid with the tip of a sharp knife.
2 Heat the olive oil in a wok or large, non-stick frying pan over a high heat. Stir-fry the squid pieces and tentacles for 1 minute. Add the chilli flakes and spring onions, then cook for another 1 minute until the squid is just opaque.
3 Add the lime juice and season with salt and pepper. Scatter the coriander over the squid and serve with lime wedges, a mixed leaf and herb salad and slices of crusty bread on the side.

CHEAT'S GARLIC TIGER PRAWNS & BEANS

This makes a tasty and filling main course, in which only the tomato and garlic dressing needs heating briefly.

1 ripe beefsteak tomato, deseeded and roughly chopped • 4 tbsp extra virgin olive oil • 2 garlic cloves, crushed • 450g/1lb cooked, peeled tiger prawns • 400g/14oz tinned cannellini beans, drained and rinsed • 1 handful of chopped parsley leaves • salt and freshly ground black pepper

TO SERVE: rocket salad and crusty bread

1 Put the tomato, olive oil and garlic in a non-stick saucepan and heat gently for 1 minute, stirring occasionally, until warmed through.
2 Put the tiger prawns into a serving bowl and add the cannellini beans.
3 Pour the warm dressing over the prawns and beans, season with salt and pepper, then stir in the parsley. Serve with a rocket salad and slices of crusty bread.

CRAB & ANGEL HAIR PASTA >

Quick, delicate and very special, crab and angel hair pasta make a fine meal, and in just 5 minutes!

450g/1lb fresh angel hair pasta (capelli d'angelo) • 2 tbsp extra virgin olive oil • finely grated zest of 1 lemon • 450g/1lb cooked fresh crab meat • 1 tbsp chopped parsley leaves • salt and freshly ground black pepper

TO SERVE: lemon wedges and a mixed leaf salad

1 Bring a large saucepan of salted water to the boil and cook the angel hair pasta for 2 minutes or until al dente, then drain.
2 In the meantime, mix together the olive oil and lemon zest.
3 Pour the lemon oil over the pasta and add the crab and parsley. Gently turn the pasta until combined, then season with salt and pepper. Serve with lemon wedges and a mixed leaf salad.

< PRAWN & THREE-PEA STIR-FRY

Super-convenient, ready-prepared ginger paste can be bought in jars from most supermarkets and Asian food shops.

300g/10½oz straight-to-wok vermicelli rice noodles • 2 tbsp sunflower oil • 4 spring onions, roughly chopped • 4 handfuls of sugar snap peas • 2 large handfuls of pea shoots • 200g/7oz/1⅓ cups frozen petit pois • 400g/14oz cooked, peeled king prawns with tail on • 2 tsp ginger paste • 2 tsp clear honey • juice of 1 lime • 1 handful of coriander leaves

TO SERVE: lime wedges

1 Place the noodles in a heatproof bowl and cover with boiling water. Stir and set aside, covered, for 3 minutes until soft.
2 In the meantime, heat the sunflower oil in a wok over a high heat. Stir-fry the spring onions, sugar snap peas, pea shoots and peas for 2 minutes.
3 Add the prawns, then stir in the ginger paste, honey and lime juice. Cook for a further 1 minute until heated though.
4 Drain the noodles, add to the wok with the coriander and toss until combined. Serve with lime wedges on the side.

SPICED TOMATO PRAWNS

Tinned cherry tomatoes are an invaluable addition to the storecupboard and one of my favourites for rustling up all manner of tasty meals; my cupboard feels lacking without them!

1 tbsp olive oil • 1 garlic clove, crushed • 1 tsp fennel seeds • 400g/14oz tinned cherry tomatoes, drained • ½ tsp caster sugar • 450g/1lb cooked and peeled tiger prawns • 200g/7oz feta cheese, crumbled • salt and freshly ground black pepper

TO SERVE: green leaf salad and pitta breads

1 Heat the olive oil in a large, non-stick frying pan over a medium heat. Fry the garlic and fennel seeds for 30 seconds.
2 Add the cherry tomatoes and sugar, season with salt and pepper, then cook for 2 minutes, stirring occasionally, until the tomatoes begin to soften and break down.
3 Stir in the prawns and feta, then cook for another minute until heated through. Serve with a green leaf salad and pitta breads.

MOZZARELLA, TOMATO & ROCKET SALAD

The secret to making this salad a success lies in the quality of the mozzarella and the olive oil – use buffalo mozzarella and a good fruity extra virgin olive oil and the results will be deliciously irresistible and moreish.

4 ripe beefsteak tomatoes, thinly sliced • 400g/14oz buffalo mozzarella cheese, drained and torn into pieces • 4 handfuls of rocket leaves • 3–4 tbsp fruity extra virgin olive oil • salt and freshly ground black pepper

TO SERVE: focaccia bread

1 Lay the tomatoes on a large platter, overlapping the slices slightly. Arrange the mozzarella and rocket leaves attractively over the tomatoes.
2 Drizzle the olive oil over and season with salt and pepper. Serve the salad with slices of focaccia.

FIG & MOZZARELLA SALAD WITH WARM VINCOTTO DRESSING >

Fresh figs and mozzarella make a sublime combination, especially if you use a wonderful buffalo mozzarella. You should find vincotto vinegar at good delis, but if you struggle, balsamic vinegar works well too.

6 ripe but firm figs, cut into quarters • 400g/14oz buffalo mozzarella cheese, drained and torn into pieces • 2 large handfuls of rocket leaves • 4 tbsp extra virgin olive oil • 1–2 tbsp vincotto or balsamic vinegar • 1 small handful of red basil and parsley sprigs • salt and freshly ground black pepper

TO SERVE: olive ciabatta bread

1 Arrange the figs on a serving platter and top with the mozzarella. Scatter the rocket over the salad.
2 Gently warm the olive oil and vincotto in a small saucepan. Season with salt and pepper.
3 Drizzle the warm dressing over the salad and scatter the basil and parsley on top. Serve with slices of olive ciabatta.

CHÈVRE TOASTS WITH CRANBERRY RELISH

Chèvre (goat's cheese), grilled until melting, goes particularly well with this tangy, fruity cranberry relish.

12 slices of baguette • 500g/1lb 2oz chèvre cheese, cut into 12 slices • 2 tbsp extra virgin olive oil • freshly ground black pepper
CRANBERRY RELISH: 250ml/9fl oz/1 cup cranberry sauce • 1 small red onion, finely chopped • juice and finely grated zest of 1 small orange, preferably a blood orange

TO SERVE: spinach, rocket and watercress salad

1 Preheat the grill to high.
2 Grill the slices of baguette on one side for 1–2 minutes until lightly toasted. Lay a slice of chèvre on the untoasted side. Drizzle with a little olive oil and season with pepper. Grill for 2 minutes or until the cheese has melted slightly.
3 In the meantime, put the cranberry sauce in a bowl and stir in the onion, orange juice and zest.
4 Place three chèvre toasts on each serving plate and spoon the sauce around. Serve with a spinach, rocket and watercress salad.

PAN-FRIED HALLOUMI WITH QUICK TOMATO SAUCE

Halloumi could have been made for this dish, but if you have a favourite cheese that responds well to being pan-fried, then give that a whirl instead. My local artisan cheesemaker produces a wonderful cheese, speckled with chilli peppers – it's hot and delicious served this way.

3 tbsp extra virgin olive oil • 3 garlic cloves, roughly chopped • 400g/14oz cherry tomatoes, cut in half • a splash of dry white wine or water • 8 small basil leaves • 500g/1lb 2oz halloumi cheese, patted dry and cut into 12 slices • salt and freshly ground black pepper

TO SERVE: mixed leaf salad and crusty bread

1 Heat the olive oil in a large, non-stick frying pan or wok over a high heat. Fry the garlic and tomatoes for 3 minutes, squashing the tomatoes with the back of a fork from time to time.
2 Add the wine and basil, season with salt and pepper, and continue to cook for a further 1 minute.
3 In the meantime, heat a griddle or large, non-stick frying pan over a high heat. Griddle the halloumi slices for 1 minute on each side, until softened and slightly golden in places.
4 Serve the halloumi straight from the pan with the sauce alongside, a mixed leaf salad and slices of crusty bread.

BLUE CHEESE, CHICORY & WALNUT SALAD

Salty blue cheese, slightly bitter chicory, crunchy celery and creamy walnuts are a match made in heaven. Gorgonzola is my own personal favourite in this salad, but do feel free to choose your own preferred blue cheese.

2 heads of chicory, trimmed and separated into leaves • 300g/10½oz strong blue cheese, such as Gorgonzola, Roquefort or Stilton, crumbled • 2 handfuls of walnut halves
DRESSING: 5 tbsp extra virgin olive oil • 2 tbsp red wine vinegar • 1 tsp caster sugar • salt and freshly ground black pepper

TO SERVE: baguette

1 Arrange the chicory on a serving platter. Scatter the blue cheese and walnuts over the top.
2 Put all the ingredients for the dressing in a screw-topped jar, season with salt and pepper, and shake until emulsified. Pour the dressing over the salad, season with extra pepper, to taste, and serve straightaway with slices of baguette.

RICOTTA & TOMATO BRUSCHETTA

Make sure you use ripe, flavoursome tomatoes and fresh ricotta from the deli counter to top these bruschetta, and the results will be sublime.

12 slices of ciabatta bread • 4 large, vine-ripened tomatoes, roughly chopped • 1 garlic clove, roughly chopped • 4 tbsp extra virgin olive oil • 5 basil leaves, roughly torn • 500g/1lb 2oz fresh ricotta cheese, sliced • salt and freshly ground black pepper

TO SERVE: rocket salad

1 Preheat the grill to high, then toast both sides of the slices of ciabatta until light golden.
2 In the meantime, put the tomatoes in a bowl. Stir in the garlic and 3 tablespoons of the olive oil. Add the basil and season with salt and pepper.
3 Place three slices of toast on each serving plate and pile the tomato mixture on top. Place a slice of ricotta on top, then drizzle the remaining olive oil over. Add a grinding of black pepper before serving with a rocket salad.

GARLIC MUSHROOMS ON ROSEMARY BRUSCHETTA >

Mushrooms spiked with garlic and served on slices of rosemary-infused toast... heavenly!

3 tbsp extra virgin olive oil • 2 garlic cloves, crushed • 900g/2lb small chestnut mushrooms • 1 handful of parsley, leaves chopped • 1 small handful of red basil leaves • salt and freshly ground black pepper
ROSEMARY BRUSCHETTA: 12 thick slices of poppy-seed bread • 4 tbsp extra virgin olive oil • 4 large rosemary sprigs

TO SERVE: mixed leaf salad

1 Preheat the grill to high.
2 Heat the olive oil in a wok or large, non-stick frying pan over a high heat. Stir-fry the garlic and mushrooms for 3–4 minutes until the mushrooms are cooked and start to exude liquid. Stir in the parsley and season with salt and pepper.
3 In the meantime, grill both sides of the bread until lightly toasted. Drizzle the olive oil over and rub quite vigorously with the rosemary, then season with salt. Spoon the mushrooms and any pan juices on top of the bruschetta. Sprinkle with red basil and serve with a mixed leaf salad.

CAPER & LEMON-BUTTER LINGUINE

500g/1lb 2oz fresh linguine, spaghetti or tagliatelle • 100g/3½oz butter • juice and finely grated zest of ½ lemon • a pinch of sugar • 2 tbsp salted capers, rinsed and drained • 1 small handful of baby parsley sprigs • salt and freshly ground black pepper

TO SERVE: mixed leaf salad

1 Bring a large saucepan of salted water to the boil and cook the linguine for 2 minutes or until al dente.
2 In the meantime, melt the butter in a small pan over a low heat. Stir in the lemon juice, sugar and capers, season with salt and pepper; keep warm.
3 Drain the pasta, return to the pan and toss with the lemon butter. Sprinkle with the lemon zest and parsley, then serve with a mixed leaf salad.

QUICK CHILLI NOODLES

Quick-cook noodles are an absolute godsend for the busy cook. Peanuts lend a gorgeous crunch and a great flavour to this family favourite – and, of course, they add valuable protein, too.

2 tsp vegetable bouillon powder • 250g/9oz quick-cook dried noodles • 6 tbsp olive oil • 3 handfuls of sugar snap peas • a pinch of dried chilli flakes • 1 garlic clove, halved • 2–3 tbsp soy sauce • 200g/7oz/1¼ cups roasted peanuts, coarsely crushed

1 Bring 600ml/21fl oz/scant 2½ cups water to the boil in a kettle, then pour it into a large saucepan. Stir in the bouillon powder and return to the boil.
2 Add the noodles, stir, and cook for 2–3 minutes or until soft.
3 In the meantime, heat the olive oil in a wok or large, non-stick frying pan over a medium heat. Add the sugar snap peas, chilli flakes and garlic and stir-fry for 1 minute. Remove the garlic.
4 Drain the noodles, then add them to the wok and pour in the soy sauce. Toss well until combined and serve sprinkled with the peanuts.

BEST BEANS ON TOAST

This family recipe makes a filling and fantastic quick dinner – it's one of my youngest son's favourite speedy meals.

800g/1lb 12oz tinned cannellini beans, drained and rinsed • 3 garlic cloves, crushed • 5 tbsp fruity extra virgin olive oil • 1 handful of parsley, leaves chopped • 8 slices of country-style bread • salt and freshly ground black pepper

TO SERVE: mixed leaf salad

1 Preheat the grill to high.
2 Put the beans in a saucepan with the garlic and 3 tablespoons of the olive oil. Cook over a medium heat for 3–4 minutes, stirring occasionally, until softened. Stir in the parsley and season with salt and pepper.
3 In the meantime, grill both sides of the bread until lightly toasted. Spoon a little of the oil over the toast and top with the beans. Drizzle the remaining oil over the beans and serve straightaway with a mixed leaf salad.

IT'S HARD TO IMAGINE SITTING DOWN TO A FRAGRANT, CREAMY PRAWN LAKSA, OR A STEAMING BOWL OF CHICKPEA, BACON & SPINACH STEW THAT HAS TAKEN JUST TEN MINUTES TO MAKE FROM BEGINNING TO BOWL. BUT WITH THE FOLLOWING RECIPES, AN AMAZING ARRAY OF FLAVOURSOME, FRESH MEALS CAN BE MADE IN NEXT TO NO TIME.

CHICKEN & BASIL STIR-FRY

Stir-frying is more often associated with Asian ingredients, but this simple, Italian-style dish of chicken, tomatoes, olives and fresh basil works really well when cooked in a wok.

400g/14oz dried orzo pasta • 600g/1lb 5oz chicken breast strips • 2 tbsp olive oil • 300g/10½oz cherry tomatoes, cut in half • 1 handful of pitted black olives • 1 handful of basil leaves • juice of ½ lemon, or to taste • 30g/1oz butter • salt and freshly ground black pepper

TO SERVE: green leaf salad

1 Bring a large saucepan of salted water to the boil and cook the orzo for 5–6 minutes until al dente.
2 In the meantime, season the chicken with salt and pepper. Heat the olive oil in a wok or large, non-stick frying pan over a high heat. Stir-fry the chicken for 4–5 minutes until it begins to turn golden.
3 Add the tomatoes and olives, then stir-fry for a further 3 minutes until the chicken is cooked. Stir in the basil and lemon juice, then adjust the seasoning to taste.
4 Drain the orzo, toss with the butter, and serve with the chicken mixture and a green leaf salad.

COCONUT TURKEY STIR-FRY

Rice noodles make the perfect addition to this simple stir-fry, soaking up the spicy, creamy, coconut sauce.

3 tbsp olive oil • 600g/1lb 5oz turkey breast strips • 150ml/5fl oz/scant ⅔ cup tinned coconut cream • 1 tsp vegetable bouillon powder • 1 tbsp red or green Thai curry paste • 300g/10½oz straight-to-wok rice noodles • 150g/5½oz mangetout • 1 handful of coriander, leaves chopped

1 Heat the olive oil in a wok or large, non-stick frying pan over a high heat. Stir-fry the turkey for 4-5 minutes until it begins to turn golden.
2 Add the coconut cream, vegetable bouillon powder and curry paste and stir well. Bring to the boil, then turn the heat down and simmer for 1 minute.
3 Add the noodles and mangetout, stir until combined, and cook for a further 2 minutes until the turkey is cooked through and the sauce has thickened slightly. Add a little water if the sauce seems too dry. Stir in the coriander and serve.

SPAGHETTI CARBONARA

The Sardinian ewe's milk cheese, pecorino sardo, is traditionally used in an authentic carbonara, but ready-grated Parmesan makes a good substitute for cooks in a hurry. Use boiling water from the kettle to speed up cooking the pasta.

6 eggs • 100g/3½oz/1 cup grated Parmesan cheese, plus extra to serve • 1 tbsp olive oil • 200g/7oz pancetta or bacon lardons • 2 garlic cloves, sliced • 500g/1lb 2oz fresh spaghetti • salt and freshly ground black pepper

TO SERVE: mixed leaf salad

1 Beat the eggs and Parmesan together and season with salt and plenty of pepper.
2 Heat the olive oil in a large, non-stick frying pan over a medium heat. Fry the pancetta and garlic for 4–5 minutes until the pancetta is golden.
3 In the meantime, bring a large saucepan of salted water to the boil and cook the spaghetti for 2 minutes or until al dente. Drain the pasta.
4 Return the pasta to the saucepan and while it is still piping hot, add the pancetta and egg mixture, then stir until combined. The pasta should be hot enough to cook the egg lightly, if it isn't, set the pan over a low heat for a few seconds – any longer and the eggs will scramble.
5 Serve the pasta with extra Parmesan at the table and a mixed leaf salad.

CHICKPEA, BACON & SPINACH STEW

Tinned cherry tomatoes make a great storecupboard standby and add a lovely texture as well as flavour to sauces, soups and stews. If you cannot find them, tinned chopped tomatoes will work just as well.

3 tbsp olive oil • 2 garlic cloves, crushed • 200g/7oz bacon lardons • 600ml/21fl oz/scant 2½ cups vegetable stock • 400g/14oz tinned cherry tomatoes, drained • 800g/1lb 12oz tinned chickpeas, drained and rinsed • 3 large handfuls of baby spinach leaves • salt and freshly ground black pepper

1 Heat the olive oil in a large saucepan over a medium-high heat. Fry the garlic and bacon for 2–3 minutes, stirring regularly, until the bacon begins to turn crisp.
2 Add the vegetable stock, cherry tomatoes and chickpeas. Bring to the boil, then turn the heat down and simmer for 2–3 minutes, stirring occasionally, until the stock has reduced slightly.
3 Stir in the spinach and cook for a further 1 minute until just wilted. Season with salt and pepper, then serve straightaway.

GARLIC & GINGER PORK

Garlic and ginger are sublime with pork. Add a little honey and a squeeze of lime, and the taste just gets better and better...

1 garlic clove, crushed • 1 tsp ginger paste • 600g/1lb 5oz pork strips • 2 tbsp olive oil • 2 tbsp clear honey • juice of 1 lime • 2 tsp fish sauce • 1 handful of coriander, leaves chopped • 250g/9oz dried egg noodles • 1 tbsp sesame oil • salt and freshly ground black pepper

1 Mix the garlic and ginger paste together. Add it to the pork, season with salt and pepper, then stir until the meat is coated in the paste.
2 Heat the olive oil in a wok or large, non-stick frying pan over a high heat. Stir-fry the pork for 5 minutes or until cooked. Stir in the honey, lime juice and fish sauce and cook for a further 1 minute, stirring regularly, until the pork is golden and glossy. Add the coriander.
3 In the meantime, bring a large pan of salted water to the boil and cook the noodles for 3–4 minutes until soft. Drain, then toss the noodles with the sesame oil and serve with the pork.

SPICY BEEF IN LETTUCE CUPS >

Choose good-quality lean minced steak for the best results. Kecap manis should be easy to find in major supermarkets or Asian food shops, but if you have difficulty sourcing it, simply use dark soy sauce and add an extra tablespoonful of dark muscovado sugar.

3 tbsp olive oil • 1 onion, chopped • 2 garlic cloves, sliced • 400g/14oz lean minced steak • 100ml/3½fl oz/generous ⅓ cup kecap manis (Indonesian sweet soy sauce) • ½ tsp dried chilli flakes • 1 tsp ginger paste • 2 tbsp dark muscovado sugar • 2 tbsp tomato ketchup • 1 handful of coriander, leaves chopped • 8 large iceberg lettuce leaves

TO SERVE: naan breads

1 Heat the olive oil in a wok or large, non-stick frying pan over a high heat. Stir-fry the onion and garlic for 30 seconds. Add the mince and stir-fry for 5 minutes until browned.
2 Stir in the kecap manis, chilli flakes, ginger paste, sugar and tomato ketchup. Cook for a further 2 minutes, then stir in the coriander.
3 To serve, spoon the mince mixture into the lettuce cups and serve with the naan breads.

CARIBBEAN BLACKENED BEEF WITH MANGO MAYONNAISE

I love to serve this Caribbean-style beef with peshwari naan, because it reminds me of the wonderful coconut roti bread found in the West Indies. Plain naan bread is a good alternative, if you can't find the peshwari.

6 tbsp olive oil • 2 shallots, peeled • 1 garlic clove, peeled • 1 tsp allspice • a pinch of ground nutmeg • a pinch of cinnamon • 1 tsp dried thyme • a pinch of dried chilli flakes • 1 tbsp dark brown sugar • 2 tbsp dark rum • 450g/1lb lean beef strips • 150ml/5fl oz/scant ⅔ cup mayonnaise • 2 tbsp mango chutney

TO SERVE: peshwari naan breads and mixed leaf salad

1 Pour 4 tablespoons of the olive oil into a food processor or blender and add the shallots, garlic, spices, thyme, chilli flakes, brown sugar and rum. Whiz everything to a paste, then transfer the mixture to a bowl and add the beef. Turn until the beef is coated in the marinade.
2 Heat the remaining oil in a wok or large, non-stick frying pan over a high heat. Stir-fry the beef for 3–4 minutes until cooked.
3 Mix the mayonnaise and mango chutney together. Serve the beef with the mango mayonnaise, naan breads and a mixed leaf salad.

LEMON & BASIL VEAL ESCALOPES >

This is a simple but stunning dish if you use good veal, so please do buy from a reliable butcher.

4 thin veal escalopes, each about 175g/6oz • 2 tbsp olive oil • 2 garlic cloves, thinly sliced • 1 handful of basil leaves • juice of 1 lemon • salt and freshly ground black pepper

TO SERVE: lemon wedges, crusty bread and herb salad

1 Season the veal with salt and pepper. Heat the olive oil in a large, non-stick frying pan over a high heat. Fry the veal for 2 minutes on each side until golden in places.
2 Turn the heat down, add the garlic and basil, then cook for a further 1 minute. Remove the pan momentarily from the heat and squeeze in the lemon juice.
3 Return the pan to the heat and bubble for 2 minutes until the escalopes are golden.
4 Serve the veal, spooning any pan juices over the meat, with lemon wedges, slices of bread and a herb salad.

GRILLED SARDINES ON BRUSCHETTA

This is a rather special version of sardines on toast, and it makes a delicious, nutritious light meal served with a salad.

16 fresh sardine fillets • 2 tbsp olive oil, plus extra for drizzling • juice of 1 lemon • 4 large slices of country-style grain bread • 1 garlic clove, peeled and cut in half • 2 thyme sprigs • salt and freshly ground black pepper

TO SERVE: lemon wedges and tomato salad

1 Preheat the grill to high.
2 Season the sardines with salt and pepper and place skin-side up in the grill pan. Drizzle a little of the olive oil over them and add a squeeze of lemon juice. Grill the sardines for 3–4 minutes until cooked through.
3 In the meantime, heat a griddle pan over a high heat. Griddle the bread for 1 minute on each side or until blackened in places. Rub the cut side of the garlic firmly over the toasted bread. Drizzle with the remaining olive oil, then rub over the thyme.
4 Top each slice of bread with four sardine fillets and serve with lemon wedges and a tomato salad.

SEARED SALMON WITH CUCUMBER RELISH

This makes great everyday eating but is good enough to serve for a special dinner, too. For a deliciously different accompaniment, I've suggested giant couscous – its moreishly nutty, pearly grains take only minutes to cook – but you could use regular couscous instead.

300g/10½oz/1⅓ cups giant couscous • juice of 1 large lemon • 4 tbsp olive oil • 1 small handful of parsley, leaves chopped • 4 skinless salmon fillets, each about 175g/6oz • 1 large cucumber, peeled, deseeded and diced • 1 handful of mint, leaves finely chopped • ½ tsp caster sugar • 4 tbsp white wine vinegar • salt and freshly ground black pepper

1 Cook the couscous in a saucepan of boiling salted water for 6–8 minutes until tender. Drain and stir in half the lemon juice, half the olive oil and the parsley. Set aside.
2 While the couscous is cooking, season the salmon fillets with salt and pepper. Heat the remaining oil in a large, non-stick frying pan over a medium-high heat. Fry the salmon for 3–4 minutes on each side until cooked but still slightly opaque in the centre.
3 In the meantime, make the cucumber relish: put the cucumber in a bowl, then stir in the mint, caster sugar and white wine vinegar; season to taste.
4 Squeeze the remaining lemon juice liberally over the cooked salmon and serve with the cucumber relish and giant couscous.

GRIDDLED SMOKED SALMON WRAPS

These wraps are great for a simple midweek meal served with a mixed leaf salad.

250g/9oz cream cheese • 4 large flour tortillas • 6 spring onions, finely chopped • 250g/9oz sliced smoked salmon • 8 sun-dried tomatoes in olive oil, drained and chopped • 1 small handful of dill, stalks discarded • 2 tbsp olive oil

TO SERVE: mixed leaf salad

1 Spread the cream cheese over the flour tortillas, then scatter the spring onions on top. Lay the salmon slices evenly over each tortilla and top with the sun-dried tomatoes and dill.
2 Fold in the sides of each tortilla, then roll up to form a long sausage shape. Cut each tortilla roll in half diagonally.
3 In the meantime, heat a large, dry griddle pan over a medium heat. Cook the wraps for 2–3 minutes, turning once, until heated though. (You may need to cook them in two batches.) Serve hot from the pan with a mixed leaf salad.

TUNA & CHERRY TOMATO SPIEDINI

Spiedini is the Italian word for skewers of meat or fish that are cooked on a barbecue, grilled, or as here, griddled. Fresh tuna is perfect cooked in this way, but do try to buy line-caught tuna. You will need 8 metal skewers.

juice of 1 lemon • 450g/1lb tuna loin, cut into 24 bite-sized pieces • 300g/10½oz cherry tomatoes • 6 tbsp olive oil • 4 large handfuls of mixed salad leaves • 1 avocado, pitted and sliced • 2 tbsp mixed toasted seeds • 2 tbsp balsamic vinegar • salt and freshly ground black pepper

TO SERVE: ciabatta bread

1 Squeeze the lemon juice over the tuna and season with salt and pepper. Divide the tuna equally among the skewers, alternating each piece with a cherry tomato.
2 Heat 2 tablespoons of the olive oil in a large griddle pan over a high heat. Griddle the skewers for 3–4 minutes, turning often, until the tuna is golden on the outside and the tomatoes are slightly blistered and softened.
3 In the meantime, put the salad leaves in a large bowl and add the avocado and seeds. Pour the remaining olive oil and the balsamic vinegar over the top, then toss until combined. Serve two skewers per person with the salad and slices of ciabatta.

PRAWN LAKSA >

This is one of my favourite quick meals because it doesn't require precise measurements and you can ring the changes with the vegetables – or even add extra, according to what you have available. Buy ready-made laksa paste from major supermarkets or Asian food shops.

400ml/14fl oz/generous 1½ cups tinned coconut milk • 400ml/14fl oz/generous 1½ cups chicken stock • 2 tbsp laksa paste • 1 handful of cherry tomatoes, cut in half • 1 handful of sugar snap peas • 400g/14oz cooked, peeled tiger prawns, with tail on • 300g/10½oz straight-to-wok vermicelli rice noodles • 1 small bunch of coriander, leaves roughly chopped

1 Pour the coconut milk and stock into a saucepan, stir in the laksa paste and cook for 5 minutes over a medium heat, stirring occasionally.
2 Stir in the tomatoes, sugar snap peas, prawns and noodles and cook for a further 2 minutes or until heated through. Stir in the coriander and serve.

SIZZLED SQUID WITH LIME & CORIANDER DRESSING

I have to admit to cooking more than the stated quantities here as I have a serious addiction to crisp, golden baby squid drenched in lime!

3 tbsp plain flour • 450g/1lb cleaned and prepared squid, sliced • 125ml/4fl oz/½ cup extra virgin olive oil • juice of 1 lime • a pinch of sugar • 1 tbsp chopped coriander leaves • salt and freshly ground black pepper

TO SERVE: seeded bread and rocket salad

1 Put the flour in a bowl and season with salt and pepper. Dip the squid in the seasoned flour to coat.
2 Heat 2 tablespoons of the olive oil in a large, non-stick frying pan over a high heat. Fry the squid for 3 minutes until crisp and golden.
3 In the meantime, pour the remaining olive oil into a small pan and add the lime juice, sugar and coriander. Season to taste and heat gently until warmed through.
4 Drain the squid on kitchen paper. Serve the squid drizzled with the warm dressing, and with seeded bread and a rocket salad.

CRISP-CRUMBED SQUID WITH AÏOLI

I love squid coated in crispy golden crumbs even more than I like the battered version that is typically served in many Mediterranean-style restaurants. For the aïoli, choose a good-quality mayonnaise.

12 medium cleaned and prepared squid, cut into 5cm/2in pieces, and tentacles reserved • 6 tbsp dried white breadcrumbs • 1 egg white, lightly whisked • 4 tbsp olive oil • salt and freshly ground black pepper
AÏOLI: 150ml/5fl oz/scant ⅔ cup mayonnaise • 2 garlic cloves, crushed • juice of ½ lemon

TO SERVE: lemon wedges, mixed leaf salad and baguette

1 Score a diamond pattern lightly across the flesh of the squid pieces with the tip of a sharp knife.
2 Scatter the breadcrumbs over a large plate and season with salt and pepper. Briefly dip the squid, including the tentacles, into the egg white, then lightly coat in the breadcrumbs.
3 Heat the olive oil in a large, non-stick frying pan over a high heat. Fry the squid for 1 minute on each side until crisp and golden. (You may need to cook it in two batches.)
4 In the meantime, mix the mayonnaise, garlic and lemon juice together. Serve the squid with the aïoli, lemon wedges, a mixed leaf salad and slices of baguette on the side.

SPICED LEMON SCALLOPS

Buy the plumpest king scallops you can find and you will adore this dish. The lightly spiced scallops are griddled and served with a warm lentil salad. If you can't find vacuum-packed Puy lentils, you can used tinned, but rinse and drain them well.

2 tsp Thai red curry paste • 1 tsp caster sugar • juice of 1 lemon • 6 tbsp olive oil • 16 fresh king scallops • 800g/1lb 12oz/2½ cups vacuum-packed Puy lentils, drained and rinsed • 1 small handful of coriander, leaves chopped

TO SERVE: baby spinach leaf salad

1 Mix together the Thai curry paste, caster sugar and half the lemon juice with 2 tablespoons of the olive oil. Brush the mixture all over the scallops.
2 Pour any remaining mixture into a small saucepan, add another tablespoon of the oil and warm over a low heat.
3 In the meantime, put the lentils in a pan with 2 tablespoons of the oil and the remaining lemon juice and heat through for 2–3 minutes; keep warm.
4 Heat the remaining oil in a large griddle pan over a very high heat. Cook the scallops for 1 minute on each side until seared on the outside but still juicy and opaque in the centre.
5 Serve the scallops on top of the lentils. Spoon a little of the spiced dressing around the scallops, sprinkle with coriander and accompany with a baby spinach leaf salad.

SCRAMBLED EGGS WITH ASPARAGUS

This is a classic and for very good reason. It's certainly a "must-eat" during the short but special season for locally grown asparagus.

250g/9oz trimmed asparagus, cut into 2.5cm/1in pieces • 10 large eggs, lightly beaten • 4 tbsp double cream (optional) • 30g/1oz butter • 8 slices of country-style bread • salt and freshly ground black pepper

1 Preheat the grill to high.
2 Bring a saucepan of water to the boil, drop in the asparagus and blanch for 1 minute until al dente. Drain and keep warm.
3 In the meantime, season the eggs with salt and pepper and stir in the cream, if using.
4 Melt half the butter in a heavy-based, non-stick saucepan over a medium heat. Pour in the eggs and cook for 3 minutes, stirring continuously, until the eggs are lightly set but still moist.
5 At the same time, grill both sides of the bread until lightly toasted, then spread with the remaining butter.
6 Stir two-thirds of the asparagus into the eggs. Top the slices of toast with the scrambled egg and the remaining asparagus, then serve straightaway.

EGGS FLORENTINE >

Crisp toast topped with lemony spinach and a golden, runny egg make heavenly eating for something so simple and speedy.

40g/1½oz butter • 4 large handfuls of baby spinach leaves • juice of ½ lemon • a splash of white wine vinegar • 4 large eggs • 4 thick slices of country-style bread • salt and freshly ground black pepper

1 Preheat the grill to high.
2 Melt half the butter in a large, non-stick frying pan over a medium heat. Add the spinach and cook for 3 minutes, stirring regularly, until wilted. Season to taste with salt and pepper and the lemon juice.
3 In the meantime, pour enough water into a shallow saucepan or deep frying pan to come halfway up the sides. Heat the water to just below boiling point, swirl it with a spoon, and add the white wine vinegar. One at a time, crack the eggs onto a saucer and slip it into the simmering water. Poach the eggs for about 2 minutes over a low heat until just set.
4 While the eggs are cooking, grill both sides of the bread until lightly toasted, then spread with the remaining butter. Top each slice of toast with some spinach and a poached egg. Add a grinding of black pepper, if liked, and serve.

MINTED COUSCOUS & FETA SALAD >

This is a wonderfully quick, healthy and delicious vegetarian main meal.

300g/10½oz/heaped 1½ cups couscous • 500ml/17fl oz/2 cups hot vegetable stock • 1 small cucumber, diced • 4 ripe tomatoes, roughly chopped • 1 bunch of spring onions, sliced diagonally • 1 large handful of pitted black olives • 1 handful of mint, leaves roughly torn • 250g/9oz feta cheese, crumbled • salt and freshly ground black pepper

1 Put the couscous in a bowl and pour the hot stock over to cover. Stir, cover, and leave to stand for 4–5 minutes until the stock is absorbed. Fluff up the grains using a fork.
2 Stir the cucumber, tomatoes, spring onions, olives and mint into the couscous, then season with salt and pepper. Add the feta and toss gently until everything is evenly combined.

CHILLI-FRIED EGGS WITH TOMATO TOASTS

Frying the eggs in chilli oil adds a little extra oomph, while rubbing the toast with fresh tomato is a simple way of adding a new dimension to toasted bread.

6 tbsp olive oil • 1–2 small dried chillies • 4 large eggs • 4 thick slices of country-style bread • 2 ripe tomatoes, cut in half • salt and freshly ground black pepper

TO SERVE: watercress and spinach salad

1 Preheat the grill to high.
2 Heat the olive oil in a large, non-stick frying pan over a medium heat. Crumble in the chillies, then carefully break the eggs into the pan. Fry the eggs for 2–3 minutes, occasionally spooning the oil over, until the whites are set but the yolks remain runny.
3 In the meantime, grill both sides of the bread under lightly toasted. Rub the cut surface of the tomatoes over one side of the toasted bread, season with salt and pepper
4 Top the toast with the fried eggs, drizzle a little of the chilli oil from the pan over. Serve with a watercress and spinach salad.

GRIDDLED HALLOUMI, PISTACHIO & WATERMELON SALAD

The salty-sweet/crunchy-soft combination of griddled halloumi, watermelon and pistachios is absolutely stunning. Plenty of freshly ground black pepper is a must.

½ small watermelon, deseeded and cut into bite-sized chunks • 2 handfuls of unsalted shelled pistachios • 500g/1lb 2oz halloumi cheese, patted dry and diced • juice of ½–1 lime • 1 small handful of mint leaves • freshly ground black pepper

TO SERVE: lime wedges, pitta breads and crisp green salad

1 Put the watermelon on a large platter, then scatter over the pistachios.
2 Heat a large griddle pan over a high heat. Griddle the halloumi for 2 minutes, turning often, until golden on all sides. Scatter the halloumi over the watermelon and add a squeeze of lime juice, to taste.
3 Top with the mint leaves and season with pepper. Serve, while the cheese is still warm, with lime wedges, pitta breads and a crisp green salad.

ROQUEFORT, ROCKET & PITTA SALAD

Roquefort is sublime in this salad, but any gutsy blue cheese can be used as a substitute.

2 tbsp extra virgin olive oil • 2 garlic cloves, peeled • 2 pitta breads, torn into bite-sized pieces • 4 handfuls of rocket leaves • 250g/9oz Roquefort cheese, crumbled into bite-sized pieces • 3 celery stalks, thinly sliced diagonally • 6 ready-to-eat dried figs, roughly chopped • 1 handful of chopped toasted hazelnuts
DRESSING: 6 tbsp extra virgin olive oil • 3 tbsp balsamic vinegar • 1 garlic clove, crushed • salt and freshly ground black pepper

1 Heat the olive oil in a large, non-stick frying pan over a medium heat. Fry the garlic and pitta for 2 minutes, turning occasionally, or until the bread is golden. Remove the pitta from the pan, season with salt and pepper and set aside. Discard the garlic.
2 Put the rocket in a salad bowl and scatter the Roquefort over the top. Next, add the celery, figs, hazelnuts and fried pitta bread.
3 Put all the ingredients for the dressing into a screw-top jar and shake until emulsified. Season to taste. Pour the dressing over the salad, toss gently until combined and serve straightaway.

PEACH & FETA SALAD WITH LIME DRESSING

This salad is full of fresh, summery flavours, and the combination of fruit, vegetables, cheese and lentils makes a well-balanced complete meal. You could try ready-cooked quinoa in place of the lentils, if liked.

4 handfuls of fine green beans, trimmed • 800g/1lb 12oz tinned green or brown lentils, drained and rinsed • 4 ripe but firm peaches, pitted and sliced • 250g/9oz bottled chargrilled artichoke hearts in oil, drained • 450g/1lb feta cheese, crumbled into bite-sized pieces • 1 handful of unsalted shelled pistachios • 1 handful of mint leaves
DRESSING: 6 tbsp extra virgin olive oil • juice of 1 lime • ½ tsp caster sugar • salt and freshly ground black pepper

1 Bring a saucepan of water to the boil and drop in the beans. Blanch for 2 minutes until slightly softened, then drain and transfer to a salad bowl.
2 Place the lentils in the bowl and add the peaches, artichokes, feta, pistachios and mint.
3 Put all the ingredients for the dressing into a screw-top jar and shake until emulsified. Season to taste and pour the dressing over the salad. Toss gently until combined, then serve.

SPAGHETTINI WITH CHILLI OIL & GARLIC

Spaghettini is slightly finer than spaghetti so cooks in less time. You could use fresh pasta if you have trouble finding the spaghettini.

450g/1lb dried spaghettini pasta • 6 tbsp olive oil • 1 dried chilli • 1 garlic clove, cut in half • 50g/1¾oz Parmesan cheese, grated • salt

TO SERVE: peppery leaf salad

1 Bring a large saucepan of salted water to the boil and cook the spaghettini for 7–8 minutes or until al dente.
2 In the meantime, pour the olive oil into a large, non-stick frying pan and crumble in the chilli. Add the garlic and heat gently for 3–4 minutes until the oil is warm and flavours are infused. Discard the garlic.
3 Using pasta tongs, lift the pasta from the cooking water into the pan with the garlic oil and toss well until coated. Served sprinkled with Parmesan and a peppery leaf salad.

PARMESAN, SAGE & PEPPERCORN PASTA >

Parmesan adds a delicious flavour to the pasta, but I also love the Sicilian ricotta salata grated over this simple dish. This sheep's milk cheese has a little more kick than Parmesan, so if you do come across it, give it a try.

500g/1lb 2oz fresh penne pasta • 30g/1oz butter • 2 garlic cloves, thinly sliced • 1 handful of sage leaves • 1 tsp pink or green peppercorns in brine, drained and crushed • 50g/1¾oz Parmesan cheese or ricotta salata cheese, grated • a few sprigs of flat leaf parsley • salt

TO SERVE: mixed leaf salad

1 Bring a large saucepan of salted water to the boil and cook the penne for 2 minutes or until al dente.
2 In the meantime, melt the butter in a small pan over a low heat. Add the garlic and sage, then allow the flavours to infuse while the pasta cooks.
3 Drain the pasta and return it to the pan. Pour the sage butter over and toss well until coated. Stir in the peppercorns. Sprinkle with the Parmesan, scatter the parsley over and serve with a mixed leaf salad.

CHILLI HOISIN NOODLES WITH TOFU

I often serve this one-bowl meal as a quick weekday dinner. Tofu, which is made from soya beans, is a great source of protein and calcium. It has the ability to absorb flavours well, so the combination of ginger, chilli and hoisin sauce creates a really tasty, healthy dish.

250g/9oz dried egg noodles • 500g/1lb 2oz firm tofu, patted dry and cut into cubes • 1 tbsp sesame oil • 4 tbsp groundnut or sunflower oil • 5cm/2in piece fresh ginger, peeled and shredded • 2 garlic cloves, sliced • 1 bunch of spring onions, chopped • 300g/10½oz watercress • ½–1 tsp dried chilli flakes • 2 tbsp hoisin sauce • 3 tbsp vegetable stock or water

1 Bring a large saucepan of salted water to the boil and cook the noodles for 2–3 minutes until just softened. Drain and rinse under cold running water, then toss in the sesame oil.
2 In the meantime, heat 2 tablespoons of the groundnut oil in a large, non-stick frying pan over a high heat. Fry the tofu for 3 minutes until golden; keep warm.
3 Heat the remaining groundnut oil in a wok or large, non-stick frying pan over a medium-high heat. Stir-fry the ginger and garlic for 30 seconds.
4 Add half the spring onions, the watercress, chilli and cooked noodles. Stir-fry for 2 minutes before adding the hoisin sauce and stock, toss well until combined and heated through.
5 Serve the noodles topped with the tofu and the remaining spring onions.

ROCKET & PARMESAN PENNE

This simple pasta dish makes a great summery meal. For a delicious variation, you could try adding a little fresh ricotta just before the rocket.

500g/1lb 2oz fresh penne pasta • 3 tbsp olive oil • 2 handfuls of rocket leaves • 100g/3½oz Parmesan cheese, grated • finely grated zest of 1 lemon (optional) • salt and freshly ground black pepper

TO SERVE: tomato salad

1 Bring a large saucepan of salted water to the boil and cook the penne for 2 minutes or until al dente. Drain the pasta and return it to the pan.
2 Stir in the olive oil, rocket, Parmesan and lemon zest, if using. Season with pepper and return to the heat for 1 minute until the rocket has wilted. Serve with a tomato salad.

OPEN RICOTTA LASAGNE

This dish shows that there really is no need to go to elaborate lengths making sauces when you're pushed for time. All it takes is a handful of simple ingredients and a little imagination.

12 x 10cm/4in squares of fresh lasagne • 600g/1lb 5oz vine-ripened tomatoes, deseeded and roughly chopped • 4 tbsp extra virgin olive oil • 1 handful of basil leaves, plus extra to serve • 450g/1lb fresh ricotta cheese • salt and freshly ground black pepper

TO SERVE: rocket salad

1 Bring a large saucepan of salted water to the boil and cook the lasagne for 2–3 minutes or until al dente, then drain.
2 In the meantime, put the tomatoes in a bowl and stir in the olive oil and basil. Season with salt and pepper, then set aside.
3 Place a sheet of lasagne on each of four plates and top with a good spoonful of the tomato mixture. Add a second sheet of lasagne. Dot three-quarters of the ricotta over the pasta and cover with another sheet of lasagne. Add another layer of tomatoes and then top with the remaining ricotta.
4 Drizzle the juices from the tomatoes over and around the lasagne and season generously with pepper. Scatter over a few extra basil leaves and serve with a rocket salad.

PIADINA PIZZA MARGARITA

Piadine are Italian flatbreads that are very similar to flour tortillas, so if you can't find the authentic version, simply use tortillas instead.

8 small piadine or flour tortillas • 125ml/4fl oz/½ cup tomato passata • 1 tsp dried oregano • 200g/7oz buffalo mozzarella cheese, drained and torn into pieces • 1–2 tbsp olive oil • 8–10 basil leaves, roughly torn • salt and freshly ground black pepper

TO SERVE: Italian-style mixed leaf salad

1 Preheat the oven to 200°C/400°F/Gas 6.
2 Lay two piadine together, one on top of the other, to make four pizza bases. Place them on two baking trays. Mix the passata and oregano together and spread evenly over the pizza bases.
3 Arrange the mozzarella on top, drizzle with olive oil and season with salt and pepper. Scatter the basil over, then bake for 5 minutes until the mozzarella has melted and is starting to colour. Serve with a mixed leaf salad.

A HEALTHY SESAME CHICKEN SALAD, WHOLESOME AND HEARTY SPICED SALMON IN NOODLE MISO BROTH, AND EXOTIC GOLDEN GINGER DUCK ARE JUST SOME OF THE DELECTABLE DISHES IN THIS CHAPTER. NOT ONLY ARE THEY A DODDLE TO PREPARE, THEY'RE ALSO BURSTING WITH GOODNESS AND FLAVOUR. GREAT-TASTING FOOD NEEDN'T TAKE AN AGE TO MAKE!

FIFTEEN-MINUTE MEALS

HOT CHICKEN STICKS WITH GUACAMOLE >

To speed up cooking, you could buy ready-sliced chicken breasts. Chilli fans might like to add a splash of chilli oil to the guacamole and diced tomato and chopped coriander also make great additions. You will need 12 metal skewers.

600g/1lb 5 oz chicken breast strips • 2 tbsp olive oil • 2 tbsp chopped coriander leaves • salt and freshly ground black pepper
GUACAMOLE: 2 ripe avocados, pitted • 1 garlic clove, crushed • juice of 1 lime • 2 tbsp extra virgin olive oil • grated zest of 1 lime

TO SERVE: tortillas, lime wedges and mixed leaf salad

1 Thread the chicken onto 12 skewers in a concertina fashion. Brush with 1 tablespoon of the olive oil and season with salt and pepper.
2 Heat the remaining oil in a large griddle pan over a medium-high heat. Griddle the skewers for 8–10 minutes, turning occasionally, until cooked and golden.
3 In the meantime, make the guacamole. Scoop out the avocado into a bowl and mash with the garlic. Stir in the lime juice and olive oil, then season to taste. Scatter half of the lime zest over the top.
4 Sprinkle the coriander and the remaining lime zest over the chicken sticks. Serve with the guacamole, tortillas, lime wedges and a mixed leaf salad.

CHICKEN & COCONUT SOUP

Coconut milk gives this soup a lovely richness, and when combined with chunky, oriental-style vegetables, it makes a hearty, satisfying soup – the perfect, easy, complete meal in a bowl.

400ml/14fl oz/generous 1½ cups tinned coconut milk • 600ml/21fl oz/scant 2½ cups chicken stock • 6 spring onions, sliced diagonally • 150g/5½oz baby corn • 250g/9oz cooked chicken breast, shredded • 1 carrot, shredded • 150g/5½oz mangetout • 1 handful of coriander, leaves chopped • salt and freshly ground black pepper

1 Pour the coconut milk and chicken stock into a large saucepan and bring to the boil. Turn the heat down, add the spring onions and baby corn, then simmer for 2 minutes.
2 Add the chicken, carrot, mangetout and coriander, season with salt and pepper, then warm through. Serve straightaway.

SESAME CHICKEN SALAD

Sesame seeds make a lovely crunchy, golden coating for strips of chicken. I also like to serve these as a finger food at parties with a bowl of sweet chilli sauce for dipping.

1 egg • 100g/3½oz/⅔ cup sesame seeds • 450g/1lb chicken breast strips • 3 tbsp olive oil • 4 handfuls of beansprouts • 1 small bunch of spring onions, coarsely chopped • 2 carrots, cut into thin ribbons • 250g/9oz cherry tomatoes, cut in half
DRESSING: juice of 1 lime • 1 tsp clear honey • 4 tbsp olive oil

1 Beat the egg in a bowl and put the sesame seeds on a plate. Dip the strips of chicken into the egg, shake off any excess, then turn them in the sesame seeds until lightly coated.
2 Heat the olive oil in a wok or large, non-stick frying pan over a high heat. Fry the chicken for 5 minutes, turning once, until golden and cooked through; drain on kitchen paper.
3 In the meantime, put the beansprouts, spring onions, carrots and tomatoes in a serving bowl.
4 Mix the ingredients for the dressing together, pour it over the salad and toss until combined. Serve the salad topped with the chicken.

GOLDEN GINGER DUCK

Keep ginger fresh by storing it, already peeled, in the freezer. There's no need to defrost it before use – simply grate straight from frozen.

600ml/21fl oz/scant 2½ cups vegetable or chicken stock • 4 tbsp orange marmalade • 1 garlic clove, crushed • 3 tbsp soy sauce • 2 tsp fish sauce • 2.5cm/1in piece fresh ginger, grated • 2 tbsp salted peanuts, crushed (optional) • 4 duck breasts, cut into thin strips • 250g/9oz quick-cook dried egg noodles • 3 tbsp sunflower oil • 500g/1lb 2oz stir-fry mixed vegetables

1 Bring the stock to the boil in a large saucepan.
2 In the meantime, put the marmalade in a bowl with the garlic, soy sauce, fish sauce and ginger. Add the peanuts, if using, then stir well. Dip the duck into the mixture and turn until well coated.
3 Add the noodles to the boiling stock and cook for 3–4 minutes or until soft, then drain.
4 In the meantime, heat 2 tablespoons of the sunflower oil in a wok or large, non-stick frying pan over a medium-high heat. Stir-fry the vegetables for 2 minutes until slightly softened, then remove them from the wok and keep warm.
5 Heat the remaining oil and stir-fry the duck for 3–4 minutes until golden and just cooked (the duck should still be slightly pink in the centre). Serve the noodles topped with the vegetables and duck.

PANCETTA-WRAPPED CHEESE WITH SPINACH SALAD

Hot pancetta-wrapped cheese and peppery spinach make a great informal dinner with a glass of red wine.

450g/1lb provolone cheese, cut into 7.5 x 2.5cm (3 x 1in) strips • 150g/5½oz sliced pancetta • 2 tbsp olive oil • 8 sun-dried tomatoes in olive oil • 4 large handfuls of baby spinach leaves • 2 tbsp toasted pine nuts • 1 ripe but firm avocado, pitted and sliced • 1 tbsp balsamic vinegar • salt and freshly ground black pepper

TO SERVE: olive ciabatta bread

1 Wrap each piece of provolone in a slice of pancetta. Heat the olive oil in a large, non-stick frying pan over a high heat. Fry the pancetta-wrapped cheese for 40 seconds, turning once, or until beginning to colour and turn crisp. Drain on kitchen paper.
2 In the meantime, drain the sun-dried tomatoes, reserving the oil, and cut them in half.
3 Place the spinach in a serving bowl and add the pine nuts, sun-dried tomatoes and avocado.
4 Whisk 4 tablespoons of the sun-dried tomato oil with the balsamic vinegar, then season with salt and pepper. Pour the dressing over the salad and toss well until coated.
5 Serve the pancetta-wrapped cheese on top of the salad, with slices of olive ciabatta on the side.

LIME & LEMONGRASS PORK

Choose good-quality lean minced meat, then keep the heat high and the meat moving during cooking, and you'll get lovely golden pork that is slightly crisp.

2 tbsp olive oil • 1 lemongrass stalk, peeled, crushed and finely chopped • 1 onion, chopped • 2 garlic cloves, crushed • 1 celery stalk, chopped • 450g/1lb lean pork mince • 150g/5½oz mangetout • 150g/5½oz baby corn • 250g/9oz dried egg noodles • juice of 1 large lime • salt and freshly ground black pepper

1 Heat the olive oil in a wok or large, non-stick frying pan over a high heat. Fry the lemongrass, onion, garlic, celery and pork mince for 8 minutes, stirring regularly, until the pork is golden. Season with salt and pepper.
2 Add the mangetout and baby corn and stir-fry for a further 2 minutes until the pork is cooked.
3 In the meantime, bring a pan of salted water to the boil and cook the noodles for 3–4 minutes or until soft, then drain.
4 Stir the lime juice into the mince mixture and serve on top of the noodles.

MIGAS CON CHORIZO

Migas is the Spanish word for "crumbs" or "small pieces of bread" and, at its most basic, this traditional peasant dish consists of stale leftover bread simply fried in a little lard. However, each region has its own adaptation and this is my version.

2 tbsp olive oil • 3 garlic cloves, sliced • 3 thick slices of country-style white bread, crusts removed and torn into bite-sized pieces • 300g/10½oz chorizo picante, sliced into bite-sized pieces • 200g/7oz roasted peppers in olive oil, drained and sliced • 1 small bunch of flat-leaf parsley, leaves chopped • salt and freshly ground black pepper

TO SERVE: peppery mizuna salad

1 Heat the olive oil in a large, non-stick frying pan over a low heat. Fry the garlic for 2 minutes until the oil is infused with the garlic. Add the bread, turn the heat up a little, and fry for 3–4 minutes until golden all over.
2 Stir in the chorizo and cook for 3–4 minutes, stirring frequently, until the chorizo is hot and sizzling. Toss in the peppers and cook for a further 1 minute. Season with salt and pepper, then sprinkle the parsley over the top. Serve with a mizuna salad.

BUTTER BEAN & CHORIZO PAN-FRY >

Butter beans and piquant chorizo make great partners in this speedy dinner, which needs nothing more than some good crusty bread and a green salad to make a satisfying and tasty meal.

3 tbsp olive oil • 1 onion, finely chopped • 800g/1lb 12oz tinned chopped tomatoes, strained • ½ tsp caster sugar • 800g/1lb 12oz tinned butter beans, drained and rinsed • 225g/8oz sliced or diced chorizo • a few flat leaf parsley sprigs • salt and freshly ground black pepper

TO SERVE: crisp green salad and crusty bread

1 Heat the oil in a large, non-stick frying pan over a medium heat. Fry the onion for 2–3 minutes, stirring regularly, until starting to soften.
2 Add the tomatoes and sugar, season with salt and pepper, then stir in the butter beans and chorizo. Bring to the boil, then turn the heat down and simmer for 10 minutes, stirring occasionally, until reduced and thickened.
3 Scatter the parsley over the top and serve with a crisp green salad and slices of crusty bread.

HERBY PORK SKEWERS

These tasty skewers are cooked in a griddle pan, but they also make great barbecue food. Chicken is equally delicious prepared in this way. You will need 16 metal skewers.

4 thin boneless pork steaks, each about 175g/6oz, fat trimmed, and each cut into 4 long strips
• 4 tbsp olive oil • 2 garlic cloves, crushed
• 2 tbsp chopped rosemary leaves • juice and finely grated zest of 1 lemon • salt and freshly ground black pepper

TO SERVE: rocket salad and flatbreads

1 Thread the pork onto 16 skewers in a concertina fashion and place in a shallow dish.
2 Mix 3 tablespoons of the olive oil with the garlic, rosemary, juice and lemon zest, then pour the mixture over the pork. Season with a little salt and pepper and turn until coated.
3 Heat the remaining oil in a large griddle pan over a high heat. Griddle the skewers for 3 minutes on each side until cooked through. (You may need to cook them in two batches.) Serve with a rocket salad and flatbreads.

< LAMB STEAKS WITH BLACKBERRY SAUCE

Tangy blackberry jam and rich, sweet balsamic vinegar make an unusual accompaniment for lamb, but the gorgeous fruity flavours make a really sublime, moreish sauce.

450g/1lb baby new potatoes • 4 boneless lamb steaks, each about 175g/6oz • 2 tbsp olive oil
• 1 tsp thyme leaves • 4 tbsp balsamic vinegar
• 2 tbsp blackberry jam, or to taste • 15g/½oz butter • 400g/14oz broccoli florets • 1 tbsp chopped parsley leaves • salt and freshly ground black pepper

1 Cook the new potatoes in boiling salted water for 12–14 minutes or until tender, then drain.
2 In the meantime, brush the lamb steaks with the olive oil, season with salt and pepper and sprinkle with the thyme. Heat a large griddle pan over a medium-high heat. Griddle the lamb for 2–3 minutes on each side, or until cooked to your liking.
3 Remove the pan from the heat and stir in the balsamic vinegar, jam and 2 tablespoons water. Turn the heat down to low and return the pan to the heat. Allow to bubble for 1 minute, then add the butter and stir until the sauce is glossy and smooth.
4 While the lamb and sauce are cooking, steam the broccoli for 4–5 minutes until just tender.
5 Serve the lamb and blackberry sauce with the broccoli and new potatoes. Sprinkle the parsley over the potatoes.

STEAK WITH MARSALA MUSTARD CREAM

Marsala, cream and wholegrain mustard make a fabulously tasty quick sauce to accompany tender fillet steak.

4 fillet steaks, each about 175g/6oz • 4 tbsp olive oil • 4 tbsp Marsala • 150ml/5fl oz/scant ⅔ cup double cream • 1 tbsp wholegrain mustard, or to taste • 1kg/2lb 4oz spinach leaves, washed • juice of ½ lemon • salt and freshly ground black pepper

TO SERVE: sun-dried tomato ciabatta rolls

1 Brush the steaks with half the olive oil and season with salt and pepper. Heat a large griddle pan or large, non-stick frying pan over a high heat. Griddle the steaks for 2–3 minutes on each side, or until cooked to your liking. Remove from the pan and keep warm.
2 Pour the Marsala into the pan and scrape up any sticky bits with a wooden spoon. Bubble for 1 minute over a medium heat, then stir in the cream and mustard. Season to taste, then return the steaks briefly to the pan, spooning the sauce over the top.
3 In the meantime, heat the remaining olive oil in a wok or large, non-stick frying pan over a high heat. Stir-fry the spinach for 3–4 minutes until wilted. Drain off any excess liquid, then squeeze in the lemon juice and season to taste.
4 Serve the steaks with the sauce spooned over, accompanied by the spinach and ciabatta rolls.

TROUT & LENTILS IN WARM CITRUS DRESSING

This dish also works with smoked trout fillets, in which case serve the dressing without heating it.

150ml/5fl oz/scant ⅔ cup extra virgin olive oil • juice of 1 small orange • juice of ⅓ lemon • 1 tsp clear honey, such as chestnut • 1 shallot, chopped • ½ fennel bulb, trimmed and finely chopped • 8 trout fillets, each about 125g/4½oz • 800g/1lb 12oz tinned cooked Puy lentils, drained • 1 tbsp balsamic vinegar • 1 tbsp chopped parsley leaves • salt and freshly ground black pepper

TO SERVE: green leaf salad

1 Pour two-thirds of the olive oil into a small saucepan. Add the orange and lemon juice and honey. Stir in the shallot and fennel, season with salt and pepper and set over a low heat to warm gently.
2 In the meantime, season the trout fillets. Heat 1 tablespoon of the olive oil in a large, non-stick frying pan over a medium heat. Cook the trout for 1 minute on each side until just cooked.
3 While the trout is cooking, put the lentils in a pan with the remaining olive oil and balsamic vinegar. Warm over a low heat, stirring occasionally, until heated through. Stir in the parsley.
4 Serve the trout on top of the lentils with the dressing drizzled over, and with a green leaf salad.

SEARED TUNA WITH TOMATO & OLIVE SAUCE

Tuna cooks very quickly; in fact it should be served pink in the middle. This is the perfect dish for a weekend meal or a dinner party, and without the need to spend hours in the kitchen.

4 tuna steaks, each about 200g/7oz • 4 tbsp olive oil • 1 lemon, thinly sliced • 250g/9oz cherry tomatoes • a pinch of caster sugar • 2 tbsp salted capers, drained and rinsed • 100g/3½oz/¾ cup pitted black olives • salt and freshly ground black pepper

TO SERVE: watercress salad and crusty bread

1 Season the tuna with salt and pepper. Heat half the olive oil in a large, non-stick frying pan over a high heat. Sear the tuna for 1–2 minutes on each side, depending on the thickness of the steaks. (Take care not to overcook the fish – it can dry out very quickly.) Remove the tuna from the pan, set aside on a plate, and cover to keep warm.
2 Add the lemon slices to the pan and cook for 2–3 minutes until slightly caramelized. Stir in the tomatoes, sugar, capers and olives, then cook for a further 5 minutes, stirring often.
3 Return the tuna to the pan and heat through for 1 minute. Serve the tuna and sauce with a watercress salad and slices of crusty bread.

CRISPY FISH WITH AVOCADO SALSA

Semolina adds a delightful crunch and golden colour to white fish fillets – choose cod, haddock or ling, in fact, whatever looks good and fresh when you're shopping. A bag of crisp oriental salad leaves such as mizuna, green mustard, pak choi and tatsoi would make a great match for the fish and juicy salsa.

4 tbsp fine semolina • 4 firm white fish fillets, each about 175g/6oz • 4 tbsp extra virgin olive oil • salt and freshly ground black pepper
AVOCADO SALSA: 1 small red onion, diced • 2 tomatoes, deseeded and diced • 2 avocados, pitted and diced • juice of 1 lime • 1 small bunch of coriander, leaves roughly chopped

TO SERVE: oriental leaf salad and ciabatta bread

1 Put the semolina on a plate and season with salt and pepper. Lightly dust both sides of the fish fillets in the semolina to coat.
2 Heat half the olive oil in a large, non-stick frying pan over a medium heat. Fry the fish for 2 minutes on each side until golden and cooked through. Drain on kitchen paper.
3 In the meantime, make the salsa. Put the onion, tomatoes and avocados in a bowl. Stir in the remaining olive oil, the lime juice and coriander, then season to taste. Serve the fish with the avocado salsa, and with an oriental leaf salad and slices of ciabatta on the side.

< SEARED SALMON, FENNEL & SUGAR SNAP SALAD

Grapefruit is typically considered a breakfast food, but here it is the foundation of a delicious sweet-sour dressing. I think you'll be pleasantly surprised by its zingy flavour, which goes particularly well with this salmon salad.

4 skinless salmon fillets, each about 175g/6oz • 125ml/4fl oz/½ cup extra virgin olive oil • 2 fennel bulbs, trimmed and thinly sliced • 2 celery stalks, trimmed and thinly sliced diagonally • 300g/10½oz sugar snap peas, cut in half diagonally • juice of 1 pink grapefruit • 1 tsp clear honey, or to taste • salt and freshly ground black pepper

TO SERVE: sourdough bread

1 Season the salmon with salt and pepper. Heat 2 tablespoons of the olive oil in a large, non-stick frying pan over a high heat. Sear the salmon for 3–4 minutes on each side, depending on the thickness of the fillets, until cooked but still slightly opaque in the centre. Cut each fillet into slices.
2 In the meantime, put the fennel, celery and sugar snap peas in a serving bowl. Whisk the remaining olive oil with the grapefruit juice and honey, then season to taste. Spoon the dressing over the salad and toss until combined.
3 Serve the salad topped with the seared salmon and slices of sourdough bread on the side.

GRIDDLED SALMON WITH COCONUT SPINACH

Succulent salmon fillets marry particularly well with the creamy, coconut-bathed spinach.

4 salmon fillets, each about 175g/6oz • 3 tbsp olive oil • juice of 1 small lemon • 2 garlic cloves, sliced • 800g/1lb 12oz baby spinach leaves • 100ml/3½fl oz/generous ⅓ cup tinned coconut cream • ½ tsp mild curry paste • salt and freshly ground black pepper

TO SERVE: naan breads

1 Season the salmon fillets with salt and pepper. Heat 2 tablespoons of the olive oil in a large griddle pan over a medium-high heat. Griddle the salmon for 3–4 minutes on each side, depending on the thickness of the fillets, until cooked but still slightly opaque in the centre. Squeeze a little lemon juice over each fillet.
2 In the meantime, heat the remaining oil in a wok or large, non-stick frying pan over a medium heat. Stir-fry the garlic for 1 minute. Add the spinach and stir-fry for 1–2 minutes until it starts to wilt.
3 Mix the coconut cream and curry paste together, then spoon it over the spinach. Stir until combined and cook for 2 minutes until heated through, then season to taste. Serve the salmon with the coconut spinach and naan breads on the side.

BAKED EGGS IN SMOKED SALMON CUPS

Eggs and smoked salmon are famously well matched. This makes a tempting, simple dinner.

15g/½oz softened butter • 4 large slices of smoked salmon • 4 large eggs • 4 heaped tbsp mascarpone cheese • salt and freshly ground black pepper

TO SERVE: spinach salad and seeded bread

1 Preheat the oven to 200°C/400°F/Gas 6.
2 Grease 4 large ramekins with the butter and line each one with a slice of smoked salmon.
3 Break an egg into each ramekin. Dot the mascarpone evenly across the surface of the eggs, and season with salt and pepper. Bake for 10 minutes or until lightly set. Serve with a spinach salad and slices of seeded bread.

FISH IN CHILLI BROTH >

Flaky fish in a light, piquant broth, topped with crispy capers... delicious!

4 tbsp olive oil • 1 onion, chopped • ½ fennel bulb, chopped • 1 tsp dried chilli flakes • 600ml/21fl oz/ scant 2½ cups vegetable stock • 400g/14oz tinned chopped tomatoes, strained • 1 handful of parsley, leaves chopped • 4 skinless white fish fillets, such as cod or haddock, each about 175g/6oz • 2 tbsp salted capers, drained and rinsed • salt and freshly ground black pepper

TO SERVE: crusty bread

1 Heat 2 tablespoons of the olive oil in a large, deep, non-stick frying pan over a medium heat. Fry the onion and fennel for 3 minutes until softened. Stir in the chilli flakes.
2 Add the stock, tomatoes and three-quarters of the parsley to the pan and season with salt and pepper. Bring to the boil, then cook over a high heat for 3 minutes, stirring occasionally.
3 Gently place the fish in the pan. Turn the heat down and cook for 4–5 minutes, depending on the thickness of the fillets, until just cooked.
4 In the meantime, heat the remaining oil in a small, non-stick frying pan and add the capers. Fry for 2 minutes over a medium heat until golden and crisp. Drain on kitchen paper.
5 Place a fish fillet in each of four shallow soup bowls and spoon the broth over and around. Top with the capers, scatter the remaining parsley over, and serve with slices of crusty bread.

< OPEN SARDINE PIADINA

Piadina is an Italian-style flatbread and a speciality of the Emiglia Romana region, but flour tortillas would make a good substitute. Ask your fishmonger to prepare the sardines for you.

8 butterflied and boned sardines • 3 tbsp olive oil • juice of 1 lemon • 4 small piadine or flour tortillas • 1 red onion, thinly sliced • 12 cherry tomatoes, cut in half • 1 handful of pitted black olives • 1 small handful of parsley, leaves chopped • salt and freshly ground black pepper

TO SERVE: lemon wedges and mixed leaf salad with herbs

1 Preheat the grill to high.
2 Arrange the sardines, skin-side down, in the grill pan, then drizzle with olive oil and half the lemon juice. Grill for 3–4 minutes until cooked, then remove and keep warm.
3 Place the piadine or tortillas under the grill for 1 minute to warm through.
4 Scatter half the onion over the warm piadine and top with the tomatoes and olives. Lay the sardine fillets on top and squeeze the remaining lemon juice over them. Season with salt and pepper. Finish with a scattering of the remaining onion and parsley. Serve with lemon wedges and a mixed leaf and herb salad.

SPICED SALMON IN NOODLE MISO BROTH

Use your favourite mild curry powder here – anything too hot will overpower the delicate flavours of the salmon and the miso broth. I sometimes garnish this dish with the crisp fried shallots that you can buy in Asian grocers.

3 tbsp plain flour • 1 tbsp mild curry powder • 4 fillets salmon, each about 175g/6oz • 1 egg white, beaten • 4 tbsp sunflower oil • 3 tbsp miso paste • 2 celery stalks, sliced diagonally • 1 bunch of spring onions, sliced diagonally • 1 small red chilli, deseeded and thinly sliced • 250g/9oz dried egg noodles • 1 handful of coriander, leaves chopped • salt and freshly ground black pepper

1 Mix the flour and curry powder together on a plate, then season with salt and pepper. Brush the salmon fillets lightly with egg white and dust them in the spiced flour to coat.
2 Heat the sunflower oil in a large, non-stick frying pan over a medium heat. Fry the salmon for 3–4 minutes on each side, depending on the thickness of the fillets, until cooked but still slightly opaque in the centre.
3 In the meantime, mix the miso paste with 900ml/ 31fl oz/3¾ cups just-boiled water from a kettle in a large saucepan. Add the celery, spring onions and chilli and bring to the boil. Drop in the noodles, stir, and cook for 3–4 minutes or until soft. Stir in the coriander. Serve the noodle broth topped with the salmon.

MOROCCAN-SPICED KING PRAWNS

The spicy marinade for the prawns is based on a Middle Eastern spice paste known as *chermoula*. It would also work well with chicken and fish.

300g/10½oz/heaped 1½ cups couscous • 500ml/ 17fl oz/2 cups hot vegetable stock • 2 tbsp chopped parsley leaves • 3 tbsp cumin seeds • 1 tbsp coriander seeds • 1 tbsp paprika • 1 tbsp ground ginger • a pinch of chilli flakes, or to taste • 2 garlic cloves, peeled • 6 tbsp olive oil • juice of 2 lemons • 1 tsp caster sugar • 1kg/2lb 4oz peeled raw king prawns • salt and freshly ground black pepper

TO SERVE: mixed leaf salad

1 Put the couscous in a bowl and pour the hot stock over to cover. Stir, cover, and leave to stand for 4–5 minutes until the stock is absorbed. Fluff up the grains using a fork and stir in the parsley. Leave to stand for a few minutes.
2 In the meantime, toast the cumin and coriander seeds in a large, dry, non-stick frying pan for 1 minute until lightly fragrant, then transfer to a mini blender. Add the remaining spices, garlic and 2 tablespoons of the olive oil and blend to a paste. Stir in the lemon juice and sugar, then season with salt and pepper.
3 Put the prawns in a large bowl and spoon the spice paste over the top. Toss well to coat.
4 Heat the remaining oil in the frying pan over a medium heat. Fry the prawns for 3–4 minutes until pink and cooked. Drain on kitchen paper and serve with the couscous and a mixed leaf salad.

THAI PRAWN & PINEAPPLE CURRY

Juicy prawns combine well with sweet pineapple, creamy coconut and crunchy green beans in this aromatic curry.

250g/9oz/1¼ cups jasmine rice • 2 tbsp olive oil • 2 garlic cloves, crushed • 1 onion, finely chopped • 150ml/5fl oz/scant ⅔ cup tinned coconut cream • 150ml/5fl oz/scant ⅔ cup vegetable stock • 1 tbsp Thai curry paste • 1–2 tbsp tomato ketchup • 100g/3½oz trimmed green beans • 450g/1lb cooked, peeled king prawns • 225g/8oz tinned pineapple chunks in natural juice, drained • 1 handful of coriander, leaves chopped • salt and freshly ground black pepper

1 Put the rice in a medium-sized saucepan and cover with 600ml/21fl oz/scant 2½ cups water. Bring to the boil, then turn the heat down to low, cover, and simmer for 10–12 minutes until the rice is cooked and the water absorbed.
2 In the meantime, heat the olive oil in a large pan over a medium heat. Fry the garlic and onion for 2 minutes, then stir in the coconut cream, stock, curry paste and tomato ketchup.
3 Add the green beans and cook for 2 minutes. Add the prawns and pineapple, season with salt and pepper, and cook for 3 minutes until the sauce has reduced and thickened. Stir in the coriander and serve with the jasmine rice.

CREOLE PRAWNS

These crisp, coconut-coated prawns make a lively combo with the spicy Creole sauce.

300g/10½oz/1⅓ cups giant couscous • 1 tsp cumin seeds • 125ml/4fl oz/½ cup sunflower oil • 1 small onion, finely chopped • 1 garlic clove, crushed • 400g/14oz tinned chopped tomatoes • 2 tbsp soft dark brown sugar • 1 tsp dried oregano • ½ tsp chilli powder • 1 kg/2lb 4oz peeled raw king prawns, tail on • 1 egg white, beaten • 150g/5½oz/1⅔ cups desiccated coconut • salt and freshly ground black pepper

TO SERVE: crisp green salad

1 Cook the couscous in a saucepan of boiling salted water for 6–8 minutes until tender. Drain and set aside, covered, until ready to serve.
2 In the meantime, toast the cumin in a dry, non-stick frying pan for 30 seconds until lightly fragrant.
3 Pour in 2 tablespoons of the sunflower oil, then add the onion and garlic and fry over a medium-high heat for 30 seconds. Add the tomatoes, sugar, oregano and chilli. Season with salt and pepper.
4 Bring to the boil, then turn the heat down to medium-low and simmer for 10 minutes until reduced and thickened.
5 While the Creole sauce is cooking, dip the prawns in the egg white and then in the coconut to coat.
6 Heat the remaining oil in a large, deep frying pan over a medium heat. Fry the prawns for 3–4 minutes, turning once, until golden. (You may need to cook them in two batches.) Drain on kitchen paper and sprinkle with a little salt.
7 Serve the prawns with the Creole sauce, giant couscous and a crisp green salad.

WARM CARAMELIZED APPLE & GOAT'S CHEESE SALAD

There are few more agreeable combinations than a juicy apple paired with tasty cheese, especially when the apples are caramelized in butter and honey, and they come with a tangy goat's cheese!

30g/1oz butter • 2 crisp apples, cored and sliced • 2 tbsp clear honey • 3 tbsp apple cider vinegar • 4 tbsp extra virgin olive oil • 4 handfuls of rocket leaves • 450g/1lb goat's cheese log (or similar), crumbled • 1 small handful of halved walnuts • salt and freshly ground black pepper

TO SERVE: rye bread

1 Melt the butter in a frying pan over a medium heat. Sauté the apples with a pinch of salt for 3–4 minutes until softened. Add the honey and bubble for about 1 minute until the apples caramelize. Remove from the heat and stir in the cider vinegar and olive oil.
2 In the meantime, lightly toss together the rocket, goat's cheese and walnuts. Add the apples, spooning over any pan juices, then season with pepper. Serve with slices of rye bread.

THREE-CHEESE FILO TARTS

These light, crisp and golden tarts are really simple and speedy to make. If you want to experiment, try your own favourite combination of cheeses and replace the sun-dried tomatoes with drained artichokes or mushrooms in oil.

8 x 15cm/6in squares of filo pastry • 40g/1½oz butter, melted • 150g/5½oz Gruyère cheese, grated • 75g/2¾oz Parmesan cheese, grated • 115g/4oz mascarpone cheese • 12 sun-dried tomatoes in oil, drained and chopped • 8 basil leaves • salt and freshly ground black pepper

TO SERVE: fruity chutney, mixed herb salad and crusty bread

1 Preheat the oven to 200°C/400°F/Gas 6.
2 Take two squares of pastry and lay them on top of each other at an angle to form a star shape. Brush lightly with melted butter and place buttered-side down in a Yorkshire pudding tin. (You want one with large, shallow holes.) Repeat to make three more tart cases. Brush with a little extra butter and bake for 3–4 minutes until light golden and crisp.
3 In the meantime, mix the three cheeses together in a large bowl and stir in the sun-dried tomatoes and basil. Season with salt and pepper. Divide the mixture among the cooked pastry cases and return the tarts to the oven for a further 3–4 minutes until the cheese is melted and golden.
4 Serve the tarts straightaway with a spoonful of chutney, a mixed herb salad and slices of bread.

BOX-BAKED CAMEMBERT

This is just like a cheese fondue in a box… only much easier to make and fabulous for sharing. Alternatively, you can scoop the cheese out onto plates and serve with a rocket salad.

2 whole, wooden-boxed Camembert cheeses • 4 garlic cloves, cut into thin slices • 16 small, young thyme sprigs • 6 tbsp dry white wine • 4 tbsp extra virgin olive oil • freshly ground black pepper

TO SERVE: sourdough or country-style bread and vegetable crudités

1 Preheat the oven to 200°C/400°F/Gas 6.
2 Take each Camembert out of its box and remove the inner wrapper. Using the point of a sharp knife, make random shallow cuts into each cheese. Insert a slice of garlic and sprig of thyme into each slit. Return the cheeses to their wooden boxes.
3 Spoon the wine over the surface and add a good grinding of black pepper. Place the boxes on a baking sheet and bake for 6–8 minutes until soft and melted inside. Serve with slices of bread and vegetable crudités.

"POOR MAN'S PARMESAN" PASTA

In Italy, crisp, fried breadcrumbs were traditionally used as a cheap substitute for Parmesan by those who couldn't afford the real thing. I think they make a wonderful alternative.

450g/1lb dried penne pasta • 4 tbsp extra virgin olive oil • 100g/3½oz/1¼ cups fresh white breadcrumbs • 250g/9oz mascarpone cheese • grated zest of 2 lemons • salt and freshly ground black pepper

TO SERVE: green leaf salad

1 Bring a large saucepan of salted water to the boil and cook the penne for 10 minutes or until al dente.
2 In the meantime, heat the olive oil in a large, non-stick frying pan over a medium heat. Fry the breadcrumbs for 2–3 minutes until golden. Remove from the heat and season with a little salt. Set aside.
3 Mix the mascarpone and lemon zest together and season with a little pepper.
4 Drain the pasta, return it to the pan, then stir in the lemon mascarpone and heat through. Serve the pasta sprinkled with the golden crumbs, and with a green leaf salad.

FRESH MINT & PEA PESTO CAVATAPPI >

Cavatappi are whirly spirals of pasta that catch this lovely, vibrant homemade pesto, but any pasta shape would do.

450g/1lb dried cavatappi pasta • salt and freshly ground black pepper
PEA & MINT PESTO: 300g/10½oz/2 cups frozen peas • 4 tbsp extra virgin olive oil • 2 garlic cloves, crushed • 100g/3½oz/⅔ cup blanched almonds, chopped • 100g/3½oz Parmesan cheese, grated, plus extra to serve • 5–6 mint leaves • a pinch of sugar

TO SERVE: mixed leaf salad

1 Bring a large saucepan of salted water to the boil and cook the cavatappi for 10 minutes or until al dente.
2 In the meantime, cook the peas in boiling water for 2–3 minutes until just tender. Drain and transfer to a blender. Add the olive oil, garlic and almonds, then process to a coarse paste. Add the Parmesan and mint, process again, and season with a little sugar, salt and pepper.
3 Drain the pasta, return it to the pan, then stir in the pesto and heat though. Serve the pasta sprinkled with extra Parmesan, if desired, and with a mixed leaf salad.

BIG-BOWL MINESTRONE

Frozen bags of mixed veg are a great standby to have on hand – they're a boon if you're short of time and healthy, too.

2 tbsp olive oil • 1 onion, chopped • 450g/1lb mixed frozen vegetables • 600ml/21fl oz/scant 2½ cups vegetable stock • 400g/14oz tinned chopped tomatoes • 200g/7oz small dried pasta, such as ditaline, farfalline or vermicelli • 400g/14oz tinned cannellini beans, drained and rinsed • 1 small handful of parsley, leaves chopped • salt and freshly ground black pepper

TO SERVE: country-style bread

1 Heat the olive oil in a large saucepan over a medium heat. Fry the onion for 2 minutes until softened. Add the vegetables and stock and bring to the boil. Stir in the tomatoes, season with salt and pepper and cook for 2–3 minutes.
2 Add the pasta and beans, return to almost boiling point and cook for 8 minutes, stirring occasionally, until the pasta is al dente and the soup has thickened. Stir in the parsley and serve the soup with slices of country-style bread.

SPICY COCONUT & CHICKPEA SOUP

This filling and comforting soup makes a great dinner on a cold winter's night.

2 tbsp olive oil • 2 garlic cloves, crushed • 1 onion, chopped • 1 celery stalk, finely chopped • 150ml/5fl oz/scant ⅔ cup tinned coconut cream • 600ml/21fl oz/scant 2½ cups vegetable stock • 400g/14oz tinned chickpeas, drained • 2 large handfuls of baby spinach leaves • 1 long red chilli, deseeded and shredded

1 Heat the olive oil in a large saucepan over a medium heat. Fry the garlic, onion and celery for 3 minutes until softened.
2 Add the coconut cream and stock and stir well until combined. Bring to the boil, then turn the heat down and simmer for 2 minutes.
3 Add the chickpeas and simmer for 5 minutes until slightly reduced and thickened. Stir in the spinach and chilli then cook for a further 2 minutes until the spinach has wilted. Serve straightaway.

MISO & TOFU SOUP WITH WONTONS

Crisp, fried wonton wrappers make an unusual garnish for this easy soup. You may need to adjust the quantity of miso, according to the brand you are using, since some are more concentrated than others. Note that the lighter the colour, the milder the flavour.

3–4 heaped tsp brown miso paste • 1 small bunch of spring onions, chopped • 5cm/2in piece fresh ginger, peeled and thinly sliced • 200g/7oz brown cap mushrooms, sliced • 1 head of Chinese leaves, shredded • 450g/1lb firm tofu, patted dry and cubed • 6 tbsp sunflower oil • 4 wonton wrappers, cut into thin strips

1 Pour 900ml/31fl oz/3¾ cups just-boiled water from a kettle into a large saucepan and stir in the miso paste. Add the spring onions, ginger and mushrooms, then bring the soup back to the boil.
2 Add the Chinese leaves and tofu, turn the heat down and simmer for 3 minutes until the leaves have wilted and the tofu is heated through.
3 In the meantime, heat the sunflower oil in a wok or frying pan until very hot. Fry the wonton strips for 2 minutes or until golden and crisp. Drain on kitchen paper. Serve the soup topped with the wonton ribbons.

NOW THAT YOU'VE SEEN – AND
HOPEFULLY TASTED – IN EARLIER
CHAPTERS WHAT AMAZING DISHES
CAN BE ACHIEVED IN SUCH A SHORT
AMOUNT OF TIME, TWENTY
MINUTES IS GOING TO SOUND
POSITIVELY LUXURIOUS! HERE, I'VE
INCLUDED A MIXED SHELLFISH
COLOMBO FROM THE CARIBBEAN,
THAI-SIZZLED LAMB AND A SIMPLE
SWISS CHEESE FONDUE.

TWENTY-MINUTE MEALS

GRIDDLED GREMOLATA-CRUSTED CHICKEN

Gremolata is the classic Italian garnish for *osso bucco* (slow-cooked veal), but it seems a shame not to eat it with other types of dishes, too.

450g/1lb baby new potatoes • 15g/½oz butter • 4 skinless, boneless chicken breasts, each about 175g/6oz • 2 garlic cloves, crushed • 1 handful of parsley, leaves chopped • grated zest of 2 lemons • 2 tbsp olive oil • salt and freshly ground black pepper

TO SERVE: mixed leaf salad

1 Cook the potatoes in a saucepan of boiling salted water for 12–15 minutes or until tender. Drain and toss in the butter.
2 While the potatoes are cooking, use a rolling pin or meat mallet to flatten the chicken breasts slightly.
3 Mix the garlic, parsley and three-quarters of the lemon zest together in a bowl, then season with salt and pepper. Scatter the mixture over the chicken and press it into the meat until evenly coated.
4 Heat the oil in a large griddle pan over a medium-high heat. Griddle the chicken for 3–4 minutes on each side until cooked. Scatter with the remaining lemon zest and serve with the potatoes and a salad.

TWICE-COOKED CRISPY CHICKEN WITH SESAME CABBAGE

I love this combination of sticky, sweet, salty and spicy flavours that coat the chicken breasts. If I'm in a real hurry, I sometimes cheat and just buy a freshly roasted chicken.

600ml/21fl oz/scant 2½ cups chicken stock • 4 skinless, boneless chicken breasts, each about 175g/6oz • 2 tbsp plain flour • 2 tsp dark brown sugar • 2 tsp ground ginger • 4 tbsp sunflower oil • 250g/9oz dried egg noodles • 2 tbsp sesame oil • 1 Savoy cabbage, leaves shredded • 4 tbsp sesame seeds • salt and freshly ground black pepper

1 Bring the stock to the boil in a large saucepan. Add the chicken breasts and poach for 5 minutes.
2 In the meantime, mix together the flour, sugar and ginger in a bowl, then season with salt and pepper. Using a slotted spoon, remove the chicken from the pan and shred using two forks. Dredge in the flour.
3 Heat half the oil in a wok or large, non-stick frying pan over a medium-high heat. Fry the chicken for 3–4 minutes, turning once, until dark and slightly crisp. Drain on kitchen paper and keep warm.
4 Bring a pan of salted water to the boil and cook the noodles for 3–4 minutes or until soft. Drain and toss in the sesame oil.
5 In the meantime, heat the remaining oil in the cleaned wok or frying pan. Stir-fry the cabbage and sesame seeds for 3–4 minutes until the cabbage is just tender; season to taste. Serve the chicken with the cabbage and noodles.

CHICKEN ESCALOPES IN RICH TOMATO SAUCE

The combination of golden chicken and basil-infused tomato sauce is really popular in my house, and I hope it will be in yours, too.

4 tbsp plain flour • 4 chicken escalopes, each about 175g/6oz • 4 tbsp olive oil • salt and freshly ground black pepper
TOMATO SAUCE: 3 tbsp olive oil • 1 onion, finely chopped • 2 garlic cloves, crushed • 400g/14oz tinned chopped tomatoes • 2 tsp caster sugar • 1 small handful of basil, leaves roughly torn

TO SERVE: watercress salad and crusty bread

1 To make the tomato sauce, heat the olive oil in a saucepan over a medium heat. Fry the onion and garlic for 2 minutes until softened.
2 Add the tomatoes and sugar, season with salt and pepper. Bring to the boil, then turn the heat down and simmer for 10–15 minutes until glossy and thickened. Stir in the basil.
3 In the meantime, spread the flour on a plate and season with salt and pepper. Coat the chicken escalopes in the seasoned flour and shake to remove any excess.
4 Heat the olive oil in a large, non-stick frying pan. Fry the chicken for about 4 minutes on each side until golden and cooked through. Serve with the tomato sauce alongside, a watercress salad and slices of crusty bread.

BALINESE SPICY CHICKEN SOUP

This fragrant soup is based on a dish I ate in Bali. The Balinese tend to use aromatic spice pastes as the foundation of a dish, but the exact quantities of flavourings aren't set in stone. So feel free to experiment according to how mild or fiery you like your food.

2 shallots, chopped • 1 lemongrass stalk, finely chopped • 2.5cm/1in piece fresh ginger, peeled and roughly chopped • 1 garlic clove, crushed • 1 tbsp palm sugar or soft brown sugar • 2 small red chillies • 1 small handful of cashew nuts or macadamia nuts • 2 tbsp sunflower oil • 450g/1lb minced chicken • 1 litre/35fl oz/4 cups chicken stock • 3 kaffir lime leaves, shredded

1 Put the shallots, lemongrass, ginger, garlic, palm sugar and 1 chilli in a food processor and blend to a paste. Add the cashew nuts and process again to make a coarse paste.
2 Heat the sunflower oil in a large saucepan over a high heat. Fry the paste for 30 seconds, stirring continuously.
3 Add the mince and fry for a further 2–3 minutes until beginning to colour. Pour in the stock, bring to the boil, then turn the heat down and simmer for about 12 minutes until the chicken is cooked.
4 In the meantime, finely slice the remaining chilli. Stir the lime leaves into the soup and scatter the sliced chilli over the top before serving.

SAUSAGE & RED WINE FUSILLI

Cook the pasta for a little less time than suggested on the packet, then finish cooking it in the sauce so the gutsy flavours infuse the fusilli.

2 tbsp olive oil • 2 garlic cloves, sliced • 6 good-quality pork sausages (Italian, if possible), split open• 300ml/10½fl oz/scant 1¼ cups red wine • ½ tsp caster sugar • 4 thyme sprigs • 500g/1lb 2oz dried fusilli pasta • salt and freshly ground black pepper • Parmesan cheese, grated, to serve

TO SERVE: green leaf salad

1 Heat the oil in a large, deep, non-stick sauté pan over a medium heat. Add the garlic and crumble the sausage meat into the pan, discarding the skins. Fry for 5 minutes, turning often, or until browned.
2 Pour in the wine and add the sugar and thyme. Bring to the boil, then turn the heat down and simmer for 10 minutes until the wine has reduced. Season with salt and pepper.
3 In the meantime, bring a large saucepan of salted water to the boil. Cook the fusilli for 2 minutes less than instructed on the pack until almost al dente.
4 Using a slotted spoon, transfer the pasta to the sauté pan. Stir, then cook for a further 2 minutes or until the pasta is al dente. Sprinkle the pasta with grated Parmesan and serve with a green leaf salad.

CRISPY HAM SALAD WITH HONEY & MUSTARD DRESSING

This is a great way to use up any leftovers from a cooked ham joint, but it's also worth buying ham specially from the deli counter – you'll need very thick slices.

4 tbsp plain flour • 450g/1lb cooked ham joint or thick slices, shredded • 4 tbsp sunflower oil • 8 slices of ciabatta bread • 4 large handfuls of mixed salad leaves • 1 handful of cherry tomatoes, cut in half • ½ cucumber, sliced • 4 spring onions, sliced • 1 carrot, cut into ribbons
HONEY & MUSTARD DRESSING: 200ml/7fl oz/ scant 1 cup double cream • 1 tbsp wholegrain mustard • 1 tbsp clear honey, such as chestnut • salt and freshly ground black pepper

1 Put the flour in a plastic bag and season with salt and pepper. Add the ham and shake to coat.
2 Heat the sunflower oil in a large, non-stick frying pan over a high heat. Fry the ham for 3–4 minutes, until crisp and golden. Drain on kitchen paper.
3 In the meantime, make the dressing. Mix together the cream, mustard and honey. Loosen with a little water, if necessary, then season to taste.
4 Heat a griddle pan until hot. Griddle the slices of ciabatta for 2 minutes on each side until toasted.
5 Place the salad leaves on serving plates and top with the tomato, cucumber, spring onions, carrot and crispy ham. Drizzle the dressing over and serve with the griddled ciabatta on the side.

CHEESE & PROSCIUTTO CROSTATA

It's important to preheat the oven so the pastry cooks quickly. If you prefer a thinner crust, you could use ready-rolled shortcrust pastry.

375g/13oz ready-rolled sheet of puff pastry
• 2 eggs, beaten • 100g/3½oz Parmesan cheese, grated • 100g/3½oz prosciutto, torn into pieces
• 50g/1¾oz Taleggio cheese, cut into cubes

TO SERVE: tomato and rocket salad

1 Preheat the oven to 220°C/425°F/Gas 7.
2 Lay the pastry on a large baking tray and turn over the edges to form a 1cm/½in raised border.
3 Beat the eggs and Parmesan together and spoon over the pastry, spreading it evenly up to the border. Scatter the prosciutto and Taleggio on top. Bake for 10–12 minutes until the pastry is golden and cooked. Serve with a tomato and rocket salad.

SWEET SOY & PINEAPPLE PORK

Pork loin fillet is succulent and easy-to-use. Here it's teamed with juicy chunks of pineapple and a delectable dark, sticky sauce.

250g/9oz/1¼ cups easy-cook, long-grain rice • 2 tbsp dark soy sauce • 2 tbsp clear honey • 2 tbsp Shaoxing wine or dry sherry • 150ml/5fl oz/scant ⅔ cup vegetable or meat stock • 2 tsp cornflour • 2 tbsp sunflower oil • 450g/1lb pork loin fillet, fat trimmed, and sliced • 2 garlic cloves, sliced • 150g/5½oz/scant 1 cup unsalted cashew nuts • 150g/5½oz fresh pineapple, cut into cubes

1 Put the rice in a medium-sized saucepan and cover with 600ml/21fl oz/scant 2½ cups water. Bring to the boil, then turn the heat down, cover, and simmer for 10 minutes or until the rice is cooked and the water absorbed. Remove from the heat and leave to stand, covered, until ready to serve.
2 While the rice is cooking, mix the soy sauce, honey, Shaoxing wine and stock together. Mix the cornflour with a little water to make a paste, then stir it into the soy mixture and set aside.
3 Heat the sunflower oil in a wok or large, non-stick frying pan over a high heat. Stir-fry the pork and garlic for 5–6 minutes until the meat is browned.
4 Add the cashew nuts and stir-fry for a further 2 minutes. Stir in the pineapple and cook for 3–4 minutes until heated through.
5 Turn the heat down a little and pour in the soy sauce mixture. Cook for about 2 minutes, stirring, until the sauce has thickened. Serve the pork stir-fry with the rice.

SOUVLAKI WITH CORIANDER & GARLIC YOGURT DIP

These lamb skewers are served with a classic Greek garlicky yogurt dip. You will need 8 metal skewers that fit into your griddle pan.

450g/1lb lean minced lamb • 1 onion, finely chopped • 1 garlic clove, finely chopped • 3 tbsp Worcestershire sauce • 2 tbsp olive oil • salt and freshly ground black pepper
CORIANDER & GARLIC YOGURT DIP:
600ml/21fl oz/scant 2½ cups thick whole-milk natural yogurt • 2 garlic cloves, crushed • 1 handful of coriander, leaves chopped

TO SERVE: pitta breads and mixed leaf salad

1 Mix the lamb with the onion, garlic and Worcestershire sauce, then season with salt and pepper. Divide the mixture into eight, then form each portion into a long sausage shape around a skewer.
2 Heat a large griddle pan over a medium-high heat. Brush the lamb skewers with the olive oil and griddle for 3–4 minutes on each side until cooked. (You may need to cook them in two batches.)
3 In the meantime, to make the coriander and garlic yogurt dip, mix all the ingredients together in a bowl and season to taste. Serve the souvlaki with the dip, pitta breads and a mixed leaf salad.

THAI-SIZZLED LAMB

Lamb goes really well with Thai flavours and responds perfectly to being cooked quickly.

250g/9oz/1¼ cups jasmine rice • 2 tbsp sunflower oil • 1 lemongrass stalk, peeled, and finely chopped • 2 garlic cloves, sliced • 450g/1lb lamb fillet, thinly sliced • 1 red pepper and 1 yellow pepper, deseeded and thinly sliced • 3 tbsp fish sauce • 3 tbsp soft brown sugar • 1 handful of cherry tomatoes, cut into quarters • ½ cucumber, peeled, deseeded and diced • 6 spring onions, sliced • 2 tbsp chopped salted peanuts • 1 handful of mint, chopped

1 Put the rice in a medium-sized saucepan and cover with 600ml/21fl oz/scant 2½ cups water. Bring to the boil, then turn the heat down to low, cover, and simmer for 10–12 minutes until the rice is cooked and the water absorbed.

2 In the meantime, heat the oil in a wok or large, non-stick frying pan over a high heat. Stir-fry the lemongrass and garlic for 1 minute. Add the lamb and peppers and stir-fry for 2–3 minutes.

3 Mix the fish sauce and sugar together. Add to the wok and stir-fry for 2 minutes, then toss in the tomatoes and cucumber. Stir in the spring onions, peanuts and mint. Serve with the rice.

GLAZED LAMB CHOPS WITH GARLIC SAUCE

Easy and sublime...

450g/1lb baby new potatoes • 2 tbsp redcurrant jelly • 2 tbsp Worcestershire sauce • 8–12 lamb chops, depending on size
GARLIC SAUCE: 455ml/16fl oz/scant 2 cups double cream • 8 garlic cloves, peeled • 4 thyme sprigs • 2 salted anchovies in oil, drained • 1 tbsp wholegrain mustard • 1 small handful of parsley, leaves chopped • 1kg/2lb 4 oz baby spinach leaves, washed • salt and freshly ground black pepper

1 Preheat the grill to high.
2 In the meantime, cook the new potatoes in a saucepan of boiling salted water for 15 minutes or until tender; drain.
3 While the potatoes are cooking, make the sauce. Put the cream in a pan with the garlic and thyme. Bring to the boil, then turn the heat down and simmer gently for 10 minutes until the sauce has reduced and thickened. Add the anchovies and stir for a few minutes until they disintegrate into the sauce. Stir in the mustard and parsley, then season with salt and pepper.
4 In the meantime, mix the redcurrant jelly and Worcestershire sauce together and brush it over the chops. Grill for 4–5 minutes on each side, brushing with the glaze halfway through, until golden and sticky. Remove from the heat and season to taste.
5 At the same time, cook the spinach in a pan, with only the water left clinging to the leaves after washing, for 2–3 minutes until wilted. Serve the lamb with the garlic sauce, spinach and potatoes.

SLOPPY JOES

"Sloppy" refers to the way in which the filling oozes out of the bun as you eat it. Alternatively, simply serve the tomatoey mince on top of the bun as an open sandwich.

2 tbsp olive oil • 1 garlic clove, crushed • 1 onion, chopped • 450g/1lb lean minced beef • 400g/14oz tinned chopped tomatoes • 1 tsp caster sugar • 2 tbsp dark soy sauce • 2 tbsp Worcestershire sauce • 1 dried bay leaf • salt and freshly ground black pepper

TO SERVE: 4 burger buns, cut in half • 1 handful of shredded iceberg lettuce • 2 tomatoes, sliced • 2 pickled gherkins, sliced • 2 tbsp mayonnaise or ketchup (optional) • mixed leaf salad

1 Heat the olive oil in a large saucepan over a medium-high heat. Fry the garlic and onion for 1 minute. Add the mince and cook for a further 3–4 minutes, stirring frequently, until browned.
2 Stir in the chopped tomatoes, caster sugar, soy sauce, Worcestershire sauce and bay leaf, then season with salt and pepper. Bring to the boil, then turn the heat down, and simmer over a medium heat for 10 minutes until reduced and thickened. Remove and discard the bay leaf.
3 Just before you are ready to serve, toast the buns. Place one half on each serving plate and spoon the cooked mince on top, followed by the lettuce, tomatoes, gherkins and second half of each bun. Serve with mayonnaise or ketchup, if using, and a mixed leaf salad.

GINGER BEEF & CASHEW NOODLES >

Cucumber is surprisingly delicious when served hot, and its subtle flavour works well with the beef in this robust sauce. Palm sugar can be found in major supermarkets or Asian food shops.

250g/9oz dried egg noodles • 1 tbsp sesame oil • 1 small cucumber, peeled, deseeded and diced • 2 tbsp soy sauce • 1 tbsp fish sauce • 1 tbsp palm sugar or soft brown sugar • 1 tbsp rice wine vinegar • 2 tbsp sunflower oil • 8 minute steaks, cut into strips • 5cm/2in piece preserved stem ginger, chopped • 2 garlic cloves, chopped • 1 small bunch of spring onions, chopped • 2 celery stalks, sliced diagonally • 2 handfuls of unsalted cashew nuts • 2 tbsp chopped coriander leaves • salt

1 Bring a pan of salted water to the boil and cook the noodles for 3–4 minutes or until soft. Drain and rinse under cold running water. Toss the noodles in the sesame oil and set aside.
2 In the meantime, toss the cucumber in salt and place in a colander. Leave for 3 minutes to drain any excess liquid, then rinse and drain again. Set aside.
3 Mix the soy sauce, fish sauce, palm sugar and rice wine vinegar together.
4 Heat the sunflower oil in a wok or large, non-stick frying pan over a high heat. Stir-fry the steak, stem ginger and garlic for 2 minutes until the steak is browned. Add the spring onions, celery and cashew nuts and stir-fry for a further 2 minutes.
5 Add the cucumber and stir-fry for 2 minutes. Toss in the noodles and the soy sauce mixture and heat through for 1–2 minutes, turning until combined. Scatter the coriander over and serve straightaway.

SEARED STEAKS WITH ROMESCO-STYLE SAUCE

The inspiration for this recipe comes from the Spanish romesco sauce, which is traditionally made with special romesco peppers and thickened with bread and nuts. Here, I've cheated and used chilli oil in place of the peppers.

3 tbsp extra virgin olive oil, plus extra for brushing • 2 large slices of country-style bread, crusts removed and torn into bite-sized pieces • 2 garlic cloves, crushed • 50g/1¾oz/heaped ⅓ cup whole hazelnuts • 6 plum tomatoes, deseeded and roughly chopped • 2–3 tbsp sherry vinegar • 2–3 tbsp chilli oil, or to taste • 2 tsp caster sugar • 4 fillet or sirloin steaks, each about 175g/6oz • salt and freshly ground black pepper

TO SERVE: country-style bread and green salad

1 To make the romesco-style sauce, heat 2 tablespoons of the olive oil in a large, non-stick frying pan over a medium heat. Fry the bread, garlic and hazelnuts for 2–3 minutes, stirring occasionally, until everything takes on a golden colour. Transfer to a food processor.
2 Heat the remaining olive oil in the frying pan. Fry the tomatoes for 3 minutes until they just start to soften. Transfer to the food processor with the bread mixture and blend to a coarse paste. Add the sherry vinegar, chilli oil and sugar, then process again. Season with salt and pepper, to taste.
3 In the meantime, heat a griddle pan until very hot. Brush the steaks with oil, season, and sear for 3 minutes on each side for rare steaks, or until cooked to your liking. Serve the steaks with the sauce, slices of bread and a green salad.

SALADE NIÇOISE

This classic salad, which combines the flavours typical of Nice and the French Riviera, makes a great summer dish.

350g/12oz baby new potatoes • 4 eggs • 4 handfuls of trimmed green beans • 1 small handful of salted capers, drained and rinsed • 1 handful of pitted black olives • 240g/8½oz bottled roasted peppers in olive oil, drained and sliced • 6 salted anchovy fillets, rinsed and patted dry • 450g/1lb bottled or tinned tuna in olive oil, flaked into chunks • 4 large handfuls of mixed salad leaves
DRESSING: 100ml/3½fl oz/generous ⅓ cup extra virgin olive oil • 2 tbsp white wine vinegar • 1 tsp Dijon mustard • 1–2 tsp caster sugar • salt and freshly ground black pepper

TO SERVE: crusty bread

1 Cook the potatoes in boiling salted water for 12–15 minutes until tender. Drain and transfer to a large bowl.
2 In the meantime, boil the eggs for 5 minutes. Rinse under cold running water, then peel the eggs and cut into quarters; set aside.
3 At the same time, blanch the green beans in boiling water for 2 minutes, then drain and rinse under cold running water. Add the green beans, capers, olives, roasted peppers, anchovies and tuna to the bowl with the potatoes.
4 Put all the ingredients for the dressing in a screw-top jar and shake until emulsified. Season with salt and pepper, then pour the dressing over the potato and tuna mixture.
5 Arrange the salad leaves on a platter and top with the potato and tuna mixture. Arrange the eggs on top and serve with slices of crusty bread.

SESAME-CRUSTED SALMON WITH DIP >

Sesame seeds have a delightfully delicate crunchy texture and a nutty flavour that goes superbly well with the salmon.

finely grated zest of 1 lime • 6 tbsp sesame seeds • 4 salmon fillets, each about 175g/6oz • 1 egg white, beaten • 3 tbsp sunflower oil • 250g/9oz dried egg noodles • 1 tbsp sesame oil • 2 tbsp soy sauce • salt and freshly ground black pepper
DIPPING SAUCE: 2 spring onions, chopped • 125ml/4fl oz/½ cup Japanese plum vinegar • 2 tbsp Worcestershire sauce • 1 tbsp chopped coriander leaves, plus extra to serve

TO SERVE: lime wedges and spinach salad

1 Mix the lime zest and sesame seeds together on a plate and season with salt and pepper. Brush the salmon fillets lightly with the egg white and coat them in the sesame seed mixture.
2 Heat the sunflower oil in a large, non-stick frying pan over a medium heat. Fry the salmon for 3–4 minutes on each side or until the sesame seeds are golden and the fish is cooked but slightly opaque in the centre.
3 In the meantime, bring a pan of salted water to the boil and cook the noodles for 3–4 minutes or until soft. Drain and toss in the sesame oil and soy sauce.
4 To make the dipping sauce, mix half of the spring onions with the rest of the ingredients. Place a salmon fillet on each serving plate with the noodles. Sprinkle with the remaining spring onions and coriander. Serve with the dipping sauce, lime wedges and a spinach salad on the side.

FIVE TEN FIFTEEN TWENTY TWENTY-FIVE THIRTY MINUTES

LOBSTER & HERB SALAD WITH LEMON MAYO

This makes a luxurious summery meal. Buy cooked lobster from a good fishmonger and make sure it is as fresh as possible.

800g/1lb 12oz freshly cooked lobster meat, cut into bite-sized pieces • 1 large avocado, pitted and diced • 4 ripe but firm tomatoes, deseeded and diced • 4 large handfuls of mixed herb salad leaves • salt and freshly ground black pepper
LEMON MAYONNAISE: 1 egg • juice of ½ lemon, plus extra to taste • 1 tsp Dijon mustard • 300ml/10½fl oz/scant 1¼ cups sunflower oil

TO SERVE: olive bread

1 To make the mayonnaise, put the egg, lemon juice, mustard and a pinch of salt in a blender. Switch the motor on and slowly trickle in the sunflower oil until the mixture starts to emulsify and thicken, then add the oil more quickly until it has all been incorporated. Taste and add more salt and lemon juice, if needed.
2 Place the lobster meat and avocado in a bowl. Add the tomatoes and season to taste. Gently stir in enough mayonnaise to coat lightly.
3 Arrange the salad leaves on a serving plate and top with the lobster salad. Serve with slices of olive bread.

SEA BASS WITH CREAMY DILL SAUCE

This creamy sauce is given an extra kick with the chopped capers. It goes beautifully with the grilled sea bass.

450g/1lb baby new potatoes • 300ml/10½fl oz/ scant 1¼ cups double cream • 1 garlic clove, cut in half • grated zest and juice of 1 lemon • 2 tbsp salted capers, rinsed, drained and chopped • 1 tbsp chopped dill • 4 large sea bass fillets • 5 tbsp olive oil • 450g/1lb/3 cups frozen petit pois • salt and freshly ground black pepper

1 Cook the potatoes in boiling salted water for 12–15 minutes until tender; drain. Preheat the grill to high.
2 In the meantime, pour the cream into a saucepan and add the garlic. Place the pan over a low heat and add the lemon zest, capers and dill, season with salt and pepper, then simmer gently for 3–4 minutes until slightly thickened; keep warm.
3 Arrange the sea bass fillets in a heatproof dish and drizzle with 2 tablespoons of the olive oil. Squeeze a little lemon juice over each fillet and season to taste. Grill the fish for about 6 minutes until just cooked through.
4 At the same time, cook the peas in boiling salted water for 3–4 minutes; drain.
5 Heat the remaining oil in a large, non-stick frying pan over a medium heat. Fry the potatoes for 3–4 minutes until golden. Serve the sea bass with the dill sauce, peas and sautéed potatoes.

CRISPY FISH GOUJONS

Golden, polenta-coated goujons are served with a delicious caper and chive mayonnaise. Mayo is remarkably quick and easy to make, and tastes much better than shop-bought.

6 tbsp instant polenta • 4 skinless white fish fillets, each about 175g/6oz, cut into 1.5cm/⅝in strips • 125ml/4fl oz/½ cup milk • 4 tbsp sunflower oil • 450g/1lb/ 3 cups frozen petit pois • salt and freshly ground black pepper
CAPER MAYONNAISE: 1 egg • juice of ½ lemon • 1 tsp Dijon mustard • 300ml/10½fl oz/ scant 1¼ cups sunflower oil • 1 tbsp capers, drained, rinsed and chopped • 1 tbsp chopped chives

TO SERVE: crusty bread

1 To make the caper mayonnaise, put the egg, lemon juice, mustard and a pinch of salt in a blender. Switch the motor on and slowly trickle in the sunflower oil until the mixture starts to emulsify and thicken, then add the oil more quickly until it has all been incorporated. Spoon the mayonnaise into a bowl and stir in the capers and chives.
2 Spread the polenta on a plate and season with salt and pepper. Dip the fish goujons into the milk and press into the polenta to coat.
3 Heat the sunflower oil in a large, non-stick frying pan over a medium-high heat. Fry the fish for 2–3 minutes until golden and crisp. (You may have to do this in two batches.) Remove from the pan and drain on kitchen paper.
4 While you are frying the fish, cook the peas in boiling salted water for 3–4 minutes; drain. Serve the goujons hot with the caper mayonnaise, peas and slices of crusty bread.

TOMATO & CHILLI MUSSELS

Mussels are very versatile – they're delicious in creamy sauces but work really well with tomatoes and chilli too. The juice from the strained tomatoes is not used in this recipe but can be chilled or frozen for use in another dish.

2 tbsp olive oil • 2 garlic cloves, sliced • 1kg/2lb 4oz mussels, cleaned and debearded • 100ml/3½fl oz/generous ⅓ cup dry white wine • 800g/1lb 12oz tinned chopped tomatoes, strained • 1 tsp chilli flakes

TO SERVE: crusty bread and green leaf salad

1 Heat the olive oil in a large saucepan over a medium heat. Fry the garlic for 30 seconds, then add the mussels and white wine.
2 Add the strained tomatoes and chilli flakes to the pan, and give everything a good stir. Bring to the boil, then turn the heat down slightly, cover, and cook for 5 minutes until the mussel shells have opened. Discard any mussels that have not opened.
3 Serve in large bowls with crusty bread to mop up the juices and a green leaf salad.

MIXED SHELLFISH COLOMBO >

A *Colombo* is a type of curry indigenous to the French Caribbean Islands. If you can't find Colombo spice powder, simply substitute a mild curry powder of your choice.

250g/9oz/1¼ cups easy-cook, long-grain rice • 2 tbsp olive oil • 1 onion, chopped • 2 garlic cloves, chopped • 2.5cm/1in piece fresh ginger, peeled and chopped • 1 tbsp Colombo powder or mild curry powder • 300ml/10½fl oz/scant 1¼ cups tinned coconut milk • 150ml/5fl oz/scant ⅔ cup vegetable stock • 900g/2lb raw mixed shellfish, cleaned and prepared as necessary • juice of 2 limes • 1–2 tbsp mango chutney • 2 tbsp tomato ketchup • 1 handful of parsley, leaves chopped • salt and freshly ground black pepper

1 Put the rice in a medium-sized saucepan and cover with 600ml/21fl oz/scant 2½ cups water. Bring to the boil, then turn the heat down, cover, and simmer for 10 minutes or until the rice is cooked and the water absorbed. Remove from the heat and leave to stand, covered, until ready to serve.
2 In the meantime, heat the olive oil in a large saucepan over a medium heat. Fry the onion, garlic, ginger and spice powder for 2 minutes, stirring continuously.
3 Stir in the coconut milk and stock. Add the shellfish and bring to the boil, then turn the heat down and add the lime juice, mango, to taste, chutney and tomato ketchup.
4 Season with salt and pepper, then simmer for 10 minutes until the shellfish is cooked and the sauce has reduced and thickened. Sprinkle with parsley and serve with the rice.

< NEARLY CAESAR SALAD

An authentic Caesar salad contains anchovies – this is a delicious vegetarian variation.

4 eggs • 2 tbsp extra virgin olive oil • 2 garlic cloves • 2 thick slices of white bread, crusts removed and cubed • 1 handful of trimmed fine green beans • 2 Hearts of Romaine lettuces, leaves separated • 50g/1¾oz Parmesan cheese
DRESSING: 1 egg • juice of ½ small lemon • 1 garlic clove, halved • 200ml/7fl oz/scant 1 cup sunflower oil • 4 tbsp grated Parmesan cheese • salt and freshly ground black pepper

TO SERVE: lemon wedges and olive bread

1 Boil the eggs for 5 minutes. Leave to cool, then peel and cut into quarters.
2 In the meantime, heat the olive oil in a large, non-stick frying pan over a medium heat. Fry the garlic and bread for 2–3 minutes until golden. Drain on kitchen paper. Season the croûtons with salt and pepper; leave to cool. Discard the garlic.
3 Blanch the beans in boiling water for 2 minutes until just tender. Drain and rinse under cold running water.
4 To make the dressing, blend the egg in a food processor with the lemon juice and garlic until smooth. With the motor running, slowly add the sunflower oil until the mixture starts to emulsify and thicken, then add the oil more quickly until it has all been incorporated. Add the grated Parmesan and season to taste.
5 Put the lettuce in a serving bowl and top with the beans, eggs and croûtons. Using a vegetable peeler, shave the Parmesan over the top and drizzle on the dressing. Serve with lemon wedges and slices of olive bread.

TWO-PEPPER PIPÉRADE

In this adaptation of the well-known Basque dish, I think glorious runny egg yolks beat the more traditional scrambled version every time.

5 tbsp olive oil • 1 large onion, sliced • 1 garlic clove, crushed • 2 red peppers and 1 yellow pepper, deseeded and thinly sliced • 8 cherry tomatoes, cut in half • 4 large eggs • chilli oil, for drizzling • salt and freshly ground black pepper

TO SERVE: ciabatta rolls and green salad

1 Heat the olive oil in a large, non-stick frying pan over a medium heat. Fry the onion and garlic for 2 minutes, then add the peppers and tomatoes. Cook for 10 minutes, stirring regularly, until softened. Season with salt and pepper.
2 Make 4 nests in the mixture and carefully break in the eggs. Cook for 3–4 minutes until the whites of the eggs are just set and the yolks remain runny.
3 Drizzle with a little chilli oil and serve with ciabatta rolls and a green salad.

SWISS CHEESE FONDUE

Fondues are great fun and this one is simple to make. Bread is *de rigueur* as an accompaniment, but you could also try tiny boiled new potatoes. Tradition has it that anyone losing their bread in the fondue has to pay a forfeit!

300ml/10½fl oz/scant 1¼ cups fruity dry white wine • 650g/1lb 7oz Gruyère cheese, grated • 3 tbsp kirsch or grappa • 1 tsp potato flour • 1 tsp thyme leaves (optional) • 1 garlic clove, cut in half • freshly ground black pepper

TO SERVE: French bread, cut into bite-sized chunks

1 Heat the wine in a medium-sized saucepan over a medium heat until hot. Add the Gruyère and heat until the cheese has melted, stirring occasionally.
2 Mix the kirsch and potato flour together, then stir into the pan and cook for 3–4 minutes until thickened. Add the thyme, if using, and season with plenty of black pepper.
3 Rub the cut sides of the garlic around the inside of the fondue pan and set it over its burner. Pour the cheese fondue into the pan and serve with chunks of French bread for dunking.

POLENTA WITH ARTICHOKE SAUCE

This is a rich and tasty dish that artichoke fans will love. Choose good artichokes in olive oil over those in water or vinegar.

250g/9oz mascarpone cheese • 3 tbsp milk • 50g/1¾oz Parmesan cheese, grated • 540g/1lb 3oz bottled artichokes in olive oil, drained • 2 tsp thyme leaves
POLENTA: 350g/12oz/scant 2¼ cups instant polenta • 2 litres/70fl oz/8 cups vegetable stock • 50g/1¾oz Parmesan cheese, grated • 1 handful of parsley, leaves chopped • salt and freshly ground black pepper

1 Make the polenta following the instructions on the pack, using the vegetable stock instead of water. When the polenta has thickened, stir in the Parmesan and parsley, then season with salt and pepper.
2 In the meantime, put the mascarpone in a saucepan with the milk and Parmesan. Stir over a low heat for 2 minutes or until smooth.
3 Add half of the artichokes to the mascarpone mixture and, using a hand blender, blend to a fairly smooth purée. Add the remaining artichokes and thyme and stir over a low heat until heated through. Season with plenty of pepper.
4 Pile the polenta into a serving dish and top with the artichoke sauce. Serve straightaway.

CHILLI BEANS WITH AVOCADO CREAM

This delicious meat-free chilli is a great storecupboard meal that is made even better with the avocado cream accompaniment.

3 tbsp olive oil • 1 onion, chopped • 1 tsp ground cumin • 1 tsp ground coriander • 1 tsp chilli powder, plus extra to taste • 400g/14oz tinned cherry tomatoes • 1 tsp caster sugar • 400g/14oz tinned red kidney beans, drained and rinsed • 400g/14oz tinned cannellini beans, drained and rinsed • 400g/14oz tinned black eye beans, drained and rinsed • 1 handful of coriander, leaves chopped • salt and freshly ground black pepper
AVOCADO CREAM: 2 ripe avocados, pitted and roughly chopped • 6 tbsp soured cream

TO SERVE: tortillas and mixed leaf salad

1 Heat the olive oil in a large saucepan over a medium heat. Fry the onion and spices for 2–3 minutes, stirring regularly, until softened.
2 Stir in the cherry tomatoes, sugar and beans. Bring to the boil, then turn the heat down and simmer for 15 minutes until reduced and thickened. Season with salt and pepper, then stir in three-quarters of the coriander. Taste and add extra chilli powder if you like more heat.
3 In the meantime, blend the avocado with the soured cream until smooth. Season to taste and spoon into a bowl.
4 Scatter the remaining coriander over the chilli and serve with the avocado cream, tortillas and a mixed leaf salad.

CIME DI RAPE ORECCHIETTE >

Fans of slightly bitter vegetables will love the way the *cime di rape* (turnip greens) complements the almost buttery flavour of the orecchiette pasta and toasted hazelnuts in this traditional southern Italian dish. You can substitute other sightly bitter greens, such as kale, if you can't find it.

450g/1lb dried orecchiette pasta • 3 tbsp olive oil • 2 garlic cloves, thinly sliced • 575g/1lb 5oz cime di rape or kale, tough stems discarded, roughly chopped • juice of 1 small lemon • 1 handful of toasted hazelnuts, lightly chopped • salt and freshly ground black pepper

TO SERVE: lemon wedges and mixed leaf salad

1 Bring a large saucepan of salted water to the boil and cook the orecchiette for 2 minutes less than instructed on the pack until almost al dente.
2 In the meantime, heat the olive oil in a large, non-stick frying pan over a medium heat. Fry the garlic for 1 minute. Add the cime di rape and fry for 3–4 minutes until the leaves have wilted.
3 Add the lemon juice, season with salt and pepper and cook for a further 3–4 minutes until the stalks have softened.
4 Using a slotted spoon, transfer the pasta to the pan with the cime di rape. Stir and cook for another 2 minutes until the pasta absorbs the lemony flavours and is al dente.
5 Scatter the hazelnuts over the pasta and serve with lemon wedges and a mixed leaf salad.

WALNUT PESTO LINGUINE

If you have trouble finding walnut oil, extra virgin olive oil is fine in its place. Be careful not to over-process the walnuts or they will become too oily and lose their crunchy texture and flavour.

450g/1lb dried linguine pasta • 2 garlic cloves, peeled • 100g/3½oz Parmesan cheese, grated, plus extra to serve • 100g/3½oz/1 cup walnut halves • 4–5 tbsp walnut oil • 1 small handful of parsley, leaves chopped • salt and freshly ground black pepper

TO SERVE: rocket, watercress and spinach salad

1 Bring a large saucepan of salted water to the boil and cook the linguine for 10–12 minutes until al dente.
2 In the meantime, put the garlic, Parmesan and walnuts in a food processer and blend to a coarse paste. Stir in the walnut oil and parsley, then season with salt and pepper.
3 Drain the linguine, return to the pan, then stir in the pesto and heat through. Serve with extra grated Parmesan, if desired, and a rocket, watercress and spinach salad.

WHO'D HAVE THOUGHT THAT IN LESS THAN THIRTY MINUTES IT'S POSSIBLE TO ROAST RED MULLET AND SERVE IT WITH A CHILLI AND GARLIC VINAIGRETTE, BAKE A CHERRY TOMATO CLAFOUTIS, OR RUSTLE UP A THAI CHICKEN CURRY? HERE ARE DISHES THAT ARE SURE TO BE POPULAR FAMILY MEALS, YET WILL ALSO GO DOWN WELL AT ANY DINNER PARTY.

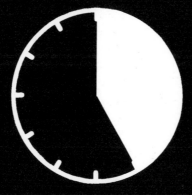

TWENTY-FIVE-

MINUTE

MEALS

THAI CHICKEN CURRY

I've used a red Thai curry paste here, but green works well too, so don't be afraid to experiment.

2 tbsp olive oil • 1 onion, chopped • 2 garlic cloves, chopped • 450g/1lb skinless, boneless chicken breast or thigh meat, cut into bite-sized pieces • 2 tbsp Thai red curry paste • 2 tsp sugar • 1 tsp fish sauce • 400ml/14fl oz/generous 1½ cups tinned coconut milk • 2 kaffir lime leaves, shredded • 250g/9oz/1¼ cups jasmine rice • salt and freshly ground black pepper

1 Heat the olive oil in a large, heavy-based saucepan over a medium heat. Fry the onion and garlic for 2 minutes until softened.
2 Add the chicken and cook for 3–4 minutes, turning occasionally, until browned. Stir in the curry paste, sugar, fish sauce and coconut milk, then season with salt and pepper.
3 Bring to the boil, then turn the heat down and simmer for 15 minutes or until the chicken is cooked through. Stir in the kaffir lime leaves.
4 In the meantime, put the rice in a medium-sized pan and cover with 600ml/21fl oz/scant 2½ cups water. Bring to the boil, then turn the heat down, cover, and simmer for 10–12 minutes until the rice is cooked and the water absorbed. Remove from the heat and leave to stand, covered, until ready to serve. Fluff up the rice with a fork and serve with the chicken curry.

GOLDEN CHICKEN GOUJONS WITH MAYO

Crispy chicken goujons marry beautifully with this herb and garlic mayonnaise.

450g/1lb baby new potatoes • 90ml/3fl oz/ generous ⅓ cup olive oil • ½ tsp dried oregano • 2 garlic cloves, crushed • 450g/1lb skinless, boneless chicken breasts • 50g/1¾oz Parmesan cheese, grated • 4 tbsp fresh, day-old white breadcrumbs • 1 egg, beaten • salt and freshly ground black pepper
HERB & GARLIC MAYONNAISE: 1 egg • 2 tbsp white wine vinegar • 2 garlic cloves, peeled • 200ml/7fl oz/scant 1 cup sunflower oil • 1 handful of mixed herbs (chives, parsley and basil), leaves chopped

TO SERVE: mixed leaf salad

1 Put the potatoes in a large saucepan with half the olive oil and the oregano. Cover and cook over a medium heat for 20 minutes until soft and golden.
2 In the meantime, make the mayonnaise following the instructions on page 98, replacing the lemon juice with vinegar and adding garlic instead of mustard. Stir in the herbs and season to taste.
3 To prepare the chicken, pound the garlic into a paste with a good pinch of salt and pepper. Rub the mixture over the chicken, then cut it into strips.
4 Mix the Parmesan and breadcrumbs together on a plate. Dip the chicken pieces into the egg, then coat in the breadcrumbs.
5 Heat the remaining oil in a large, non-stick frying pan over a medium heat. Fry the chicken for 5–6 minutes in two batches until cooked. Serve with the mayonnaise, new potatoes and a mixed leaf salad.

CHEESY CHICKEN WRAPPED IN PANCETTA

450g/1lb sweet potatoes, peeled and cut into small chunks • 30g/1oz butter • 4 skinless, boneless chicken breasts, each about 175g/6oz • 115g/4oz strong Cheddar cheese or similar, cut into 4 long slices • 8 long slices of pancetta • 3 tbsp olive oil • 1kg/2lb 4oz spinach leaves, washed • salt and freshly ground black pepper

1 Cook the sweet potatoes in a pan of boiling salted water for 15–20 minutes until tender; drain and mash, then stir in the butter.
2 In the meantime, using a sharp knife, carefully cut a pocket in each chicken breast and insert a slice of cheese. Wrap two slices of pancetta around each chicken breast to cover completely.
3 Heat the olive oil in a large, non-stick frying pan over a medium heat. Fry the chicken breasts for 10 minutes on each side until the pancetta is golden and the chicken is cooked through.
4 At the same time, cook the spinach in a pan, with only the water left clinging to the leaves after washing, for 2–3 minutes until wilted; season to taste. Serve the chicken with the sweet potato mash and spinach.

PORK TONNATO

This is a variation on the classic Italian dish *vitello tonnato* – veal in a delicious creamy tuna mayonnaise sauce. It makes a delightful dinner.

450g/1lb new potatoes • 15g/½oz butter • 4 pork escalopes, each about 175g/6oz • 2 tbsp olive oil • 6 sage leaves • 1 tbsp salted capers, rinsed and drained • 1 handful of parsley, leaves chopped • salt and freshly ground black pepper
TUNA SAUCE: 1 egg • juice of ½ small lemon • 200ml/7fl oz/scant 1 cup sunflower oil • 125g/4½oz tinned tuna in olive oil, drained

TO SERVE: lemon wedges and 4 Little Gem lettuces, cut into quarters

1 Cook the potatoes in a saucepan of boiling salted water for 15–20 minutes until tender; drain and toss in the butter.
2 In the meantime, to make the tuna sauce, put the egg in a food processor with the lemon juice and a little salt and pepper. Blend for a few seconds until smooth. With the motor running, slowly trickle in the sunflower oil. As the mixture starts to emulsify and thicken, add the oil more quickly. Once it has all been incorporated, add the tuna and blend briefly until combined.
3 Season the pork. Heat the olive oil in a large, non-stick frying pan over a medium heat. Fry the pork and sage for 4 minutes on each side until cooked through and golden. Place the pork on a serving platter.
4 Spoon the tuna sauce over the pork and scatter the capers and parsley on top. Season with a little more pepper and serve with lemon wedges, the new potatoes and wedges of Little Gem lettuce.

PORK WITH PRUNES

These juicy nuggets of pork are served in a creamy sauce with flavoursome prunes. I like to use the ready-to-eat dried variety, because I love their slight chewiness, but tinned prunes are fine.

250g/9oz/1¼ cups easy-cook, long-grain rice • 1 tbsp olive oil • 2 shallots, finely chopped • 2 garlic cloves, crushed • 8 young sage leaves • 450g/1lb piece pork loin fillet, sliced • 100ml/3½fl oz/generous ⅓ cup dry white wine • 1 large handful of ready-to-eat dried prunes • 1 tbsp wholegrain mustard • 150ml/5fl oz/scant ⅔ cup double cream • 450g/1lb sugar snap peas • salt and freshly ground black pepper

1 Put the rice in a medium-sized saucepan and cover with 600ml/21fl oz/scant 2½ cups water. Bring to the boil, then turn the heat down, cover, and simmer for 10 minutes or until the rice is cooked and the water absorbed. Remove from the heat and leave to stand, covered, until ready to serve.
2 In the meantime, heat the olive oil in a large, non-stick frying pan over a medium heat. Fry the shallots, garlic and sage for 2 minutes until softened. Add the pork and cook for 6 minutes, turning occasionally, until golden.
3 Pour the wine into the pan, turn the heat down and add the prunes and mustard. Simmer for 2 minutes, stirring occasionally, then add the cream and season with salt and pepper. Simmer for a further 3 minutes, stirring often, until the cream has reduced and thickened.
4 At the same time, cook the sugar snap peas in boiling salted water for 2–3 minutes until tender but still crisp; drain. Serve the pork with the rice and sugar snap peas.

GRIDDLED GAMMON WITH PINEAPPLE & MINT RELISH

Salty gammon and sweet, juicy pineapple are a classic combination, but add chopped mint and serve with chilli-spiked potatoes and you have a very special dish.

5 tbsp olive oil • 450g/1lb baby new potatoes, quartered • 1 dried chilli, crumbled • 4 gammon steaks, each about 175g/6oz • 450g/1lb sugar snap peas • salt and freshly ground black pepper
PINEAPPLE & MINT RELISH: 1 small pineapple, peeled, cored and roughly chopped • 2 shallots, chopped • 1 tbsp extra virgin olive oil • 1 small handful of mint, leaves shredded

1 Heat 4 tablespoons of the olive oil in a large, non-stick frying pan over a medium heat. Sauté the potatoes and chilli for 15–20 minutes, turning occasionally, until tender and golden. Drain on kitchen paper and season with salt and pepper.
2 In the meantime, make the pineapple and mint relish. Put the pineapple in a bowl with the shallots, olive oil and mint. Season with a little black pepper, then set aside.
3 Brush the gammon steaks with the remaining oil. Heat a griddle pan over a medium-high heat. Griddle the gammon for 4–5 minutes on each side until cooked.
4 Steam the sugar snap peas for 2–3 minutes or until just tender. Serve the gammon with a generous spoonful of the pineapple relish, the chilli potatoes and sugar snap peas on the side.

HERB SAUSAGE CAKES WITH CHILLI GREENS

If you can't find sausage meat, simply slip sausages out of their skins, but choose good-quality ones with a high meat content. Greek gigantes beans go really well in this dish and can be found in major supermarkets and delis.

800g/1lb 12oz sausage meat • 1 onion, finely chopped • 1 tsp dried oregano • 2 tbsp olive oil • 2 garlic cloves, chopped • 1 dried chilli, crumbled • 800g/1lb 12oz spring greens or curly kale, tough stalks discarded, and roughly chopped • juice of 1 lime (optional) • 700g/1lb 9oz bottled gigantes beans in tomato sauce or baked beans • salt and freshly ground black pepper

TO SERVE: crusty bread

1 Preheat the grill to high.
2 Put the sausage meat in a large bowl and add the onion and oregano. Knead until combined, then divide the mixture into eight and form into patties, about 1cm/½in thick.
3 Grill the sausage cakes for 4 minutes on each side or until cooked through.
4 In the meantime, heat the olive oil in a large, non-stick frying pan over a medium heat. Fry the garlic and chilli for 1 minute, stirring to infuse the oil. Add the spring greens and cook for 3 minutes, stirring regularly, until wilted. Squeeze in the lime juice, if using, and season with salt and pepper.
5 Gently heat the beans for 2–3 minutes over a medium-low heat until warmed through. Serve the herb sausage cakes with the chilli greens, beans and slices of crusty bread.

STICKY LAMB SATAY

Lamb works well with the rich, peanut sauce. You will need 12 metal skewers.

450g/1lb lamb fillet, cut into 12 thin strips • 250g/9oz dried egg noodles • 1 handful of coriander, leaves chopped
MARINADE: 1 garlic clove, crushed • 2.5cm/1in piece fresh ginger, peeled and chopped • 1 tbsp clear honey • 1 tsp fish sauce • juice of 1 lime
SATAY SAUCE: 100g/3½oz crunchy peanut butter • 100ml/3½fl oz/generous ⅓ cup tinned coconut milk • 1–2 tbsp chilli sauce • 1 garlic clove, crushed • 1 tbsp dark soy sauce

TO SERVE: spinach leaf salad

1 Thread the lamb onto 12 skewers and place in a shallow dish. Mix together all the ingredients for the marinade and pour it over the lamb, turning until coated. Marinate for 10 minutes.
2 In the meantime, preheat the grill to high. Mix together all the ingredients for the satay sauce until combined, then set aside.
3 Grill the lamb for 3–4 minutes on each side until sticky and golden. Discard the leftover marinade.
4 At the same time, bring a pan of salted water to the boil and cook the noodles for 3–4 minutes or until soft; drain. Sprinkle the coriander over the lamb and serve with the noodles, satay sauce and a spinach leaf salad.

PICADILLO WITH AVOCADO SALSA

This is my version of the spiced ground beef dish that is popular in many Latin American countries. It's often used as a filling for tortillas and tacos, which is how I like to serve it, along with this lip-smacking avocado salsa.

2 tbsp olive oil • 2 garlic cloves, crushed • 1 onion, chopped • 450g/1lb lean minced beef • 400g/14oz tinned chopped tomatoes • 100ml/3½fl oz/generous ⅓ cup white wine • 3–4 pickled jalapeño peppers, chopped • 1 handful of pitted green olives • 4 tacos • salt and freshly ground black pepper

AVOCADO SALSA: 2 ripe avocados, pitted and diced • 1 large tomato, deseeded and diced • 1 small red onion, finely chopped • 1 small handful of coriander, leaves chopped • juice of 1 lime

1 Heat the olive oil in a large, non-stick frying pan over a medium heat. Fry the garlic and onion for 2 minutes until softened. Add the minced beef and cook for 3–4 minutes, stirring often, until browned.
2 Stir in the chopped tomatoes, wine, jalapeños and olives. Season with salt and pepper. Bring to the boil, then turn the heat down and simmer for 15 minutes until reduced and thickened.
3 In the meantime, preheat the oven to 180°C/350°F/Gas 4. Mix together the ingredients for the avocado salsa and season to taste.
4 Place the tacos upside down on a baking tray and warm through for 5 minutes. Spoon the picadillo into the tacos and serve with the avocado salsa.

SPICED BEEF & GLASS NOODLE SALAD >

Although I've suggested serving the beef hot in this recipe, it is also really nice served at room temperature, so it's perfect for a summer meal.

2 tbsp dark soy sauce • 1 tbsp fish sauce • 1–2 tbsp chilli sauce • 1 garlic clove, crushed • 2 handfuls of salted peanuts, roughly chopped • 450g/1lb lean beef steak, cut into strips • 2 tbsp olive oil • 1 small handful of coriander leaves
GLASS NOODLE SALAD: 100g/3½oz dried glass noodles • 1 handful of trimmed fine green beans • 1 tbsp clear honey • juice of 1 lime • 3 tbsp olive oil • 1 tbsp fish sauce • 1 handful of mangetout • 3 spring onions, sliced diagonally • salt

1 To make the glass noodle salad, bring a pan of salted water to the boil and cook the noodles for 3–4 minutes until soft. Drain and rinse under cold running water; transfer to a bowl.
2 In the meantime, blanch the beans for 2 minutes in boiling water, drain and rinse under cold running water. Mix together the honey, lime juice, olive oil and fish sauce until combined. Add the beans to the noodles with the mangetout and spring onions. Pour the dressing over and toss well.
3 Mix together the soy sauce, fish sauce, chilli sauce and garlic in a bowl. Put the peanuts in a separate bowl. Turn the beef in the soy mixture, then press the meat firmly into the peanuts until it is lightly coated.
4 Heat the olive oil in a wok or large, non-stick frying pan over a medium-high heat. Stir-fry the beef for 4–5 minutes until the peanuts are golden.
5 Scatter the coriander over the noodles and beef before serving.

VEAL CUTLETS IN SAGE & RED WINE

This great dinner-party dish also works well with pork cutlets, but you may need to serve two per person since they are often much smaller than veal cutlets.

4 tbsp olive oil • 450g/1lb baby new potatoes, cut in half • 3 garlic cloves, sliced • 1 small handful of young sage leaves • 4 veal cutlets • 200ml/7fl oz/ scant 1 cup red wine • 400g/14oz mangetout • salt and freshly ground black pepper

1 Heat half the olive oil in a large, non-stick frying pan over a medium heat. Sauté the potatoes for 15–20 minutes, turning occasionally, until tender and golden. Season with salt and pepper.
2 In the meantime, heat the remaining oil in a separate large, non-stick frying pan over a medium-low heat. Fry the garlic and sage leaves for 2 minutes, stirring often, until the garlic is softened.
3 Season the veal and place in the frying pan. Turn the heat up a little and fry the veal for 5 minutes on each side until browned and cooked. Pour in the red wine and bubble for 4–5 minutes until the sauce has reduced.
4 In the meantime, steam the mangetout for 2–3 minutes until just tender. Serve the veal with the sautéed potatoes and mangetout.

LEMON & OLIVE ROAST SEA BREAM

The secret to this succulent roast fish dish is a very hot oven – other than that, the preparation is incredibly simple and quick. Ask your fishmonger to prepare the fish for you.

4 small cleaned, gutted and descaled sea bream • 4 tbsp extra virgin olive oil • juice of 1 small lemon • 1 lemon, cut into wedges • 3–4 thyme sprigs • 1 handful of pitted black olives • 450g/1lb purple sprouting broccoli
LEMON & PARSLEY QUINOA: 250g/9oz/1¼ cups quinoa • grated zest and juice of 1 lemon • 1 handful of parsley, leaves chopped • salt and freshly ground black pepper

1 Preheat the oven to 220°C/425°F/Gas 7.
2 Make three cuts in the top side of each fish, then place them in a roasting dish. Brush the fish with the olive oil.
3 Squeeze a little lemon juice over the fish, then arrange the remaining wedges on top. Scatter the thyme and olives over, then season with salt and pepper. Roast for 20 minutes or until cooked.
4 In the meantime, put the quinoa in a pan and cover with water. Bring to the boil, then turn the heat down to low, cover, and simmer for 10 minutes or until tender. Drain well. Toss the quinoa in the lemon zest and juice and the parsley, then season.
5 At the same time, steam the broccoli for 4–5 minutes until just tender. Serve the fish with the broccoli and quinoa.

< BLACKENED FISH WITH TZATZIKI

This is a fabulous way to prepare white fish. The lime and tzatziki create a wonderfully cooling accompaniment to the spiciness of the fish.

450g/1lb new potatoes, halved • 2 garlic cloves, peeled • 1 tbsp freshly ground black pepper, plus extra to taste • 1 tbsp dried oregano • 1 tbsp thyme leaves • 1 tsp cayenne pepper or chilli pepper • 40g/1½oz butter • 4 firm white fish fillets, each about 175g/6oz
TZATZIKI: 300ml/10½fl oz/scant 1¼ cups thick Greek yogurt • 1 small cucumber, peeled, deseeded and diced • salt and freshly ground black pepper

TO SERVE: lime wedges and mixed leaf salad

1 Cook the potatoes in a saucepan of boiling salted water for 15–20 minutes or until tender; drain.
2 In the meantime, sprinkle a little salt over the garlic and work it to a paste using the flat blade of a large knife. Put the garlic paste in a bowl and add the black pepper. Stir in the herbs and cayenne.
3 Heat the butter in a large, non-stick frying pan over a high heat. Brush the top of the fish fillets with some of the butter and scatter the spice mix over to coat. Fry the fish in the remaining butter – spice-side down first – for 3 minutes until the top is blackened and crisp, then turn the fillets over and cook for a further 3 minutes.
4 Spoon the yogurt into a serving bowl. Stir in the cucumber and season to taste. Serve the fish with the tzatziki, new potatoes, a mixed leaf salad and lime wedges.

ROASTED RED MULLET WITH CHILLI & GARLIC VINAIGRETTE >

This zingy dressing adds real pizzazz to red mullet. If you can only get small red mullet, serve one fish per person.

2 large red mullet, cleaned, gutted and descaled • 2 lemons • 2 sweet potatoes, peeled and diced • 2 tbsp olive oil • 400g/14oz sugar snap peas • salt and freshly ground black pepper
CHILLI & GARLIC VINAIGRETTE: 1 small dried chilli • 135ml/4½fl oz/generous ½ cup extra virgin olive oil • 2 garlic cloves, sliced • 2 tbsp finely chopped sun-dried tomatoes • 1 tbsp wholegrain mustard • 2 tbsp tomato ketchup

1 Preheat the oven to 220°C/425°F/Gas 7.
2 Make 2 cuts in the top side of each fish and lay them in a large roasting dish. Cut one of the lemons into wedges and arrange around the fish with the sweet potatoes. Drizzle the olive oil and a little juice from the second lemon over the top. Season with salt and pepper, then roast for 20 minutes until the fish is cooked and the sweet potatoes are tender.
3 In the meantime, make the dressing. Toast the chilli in a dry frying pan for 1 minute until slightly charred. Add the olive oil, garlic and sun-dried tomatoes, then cook over a low heat for 3–4 minutes to infuse the oil. Stir in the mustard and ketchup, the remaining lemon juice, then season to taste.
4 Steam the sugar snap peas for 2–3 minutes until just tender. Spoon the vinaigrette over the fish and serve with sweet potatoes and sugar snap peas.

MOROCCAN-SPICED FISH WITH COUSCOUS

Spice-coated fish makes a great match with buttery, saffron-flecked couscous.

300g/10½oz/heaped 1½ cups couscous • a pinch of saffron threads • 500ml/17fl oz/2 cups hot vegetable or chicken stock • 1 handful of sultanas • 1 handful of toasted flaked almonds • ½ preserved lemon, chopped • 90g/3¼oz butter • 2 tbsp coriander seeds • 2 tbsp cumin seeds • 2 tsp ground cinnamon • 1 garlic clove, crushed • 5–6 tbsp olive oil • 4 pollock fillets, each about 200g/7oz • 1 handful of coriander, leaves chopped • salt and freshly ground black pepper

TO SERVE: tomato and rocket salad

1 Preheat the oven to 200°C/400°F/Gas 6.
2 Put the couscous in an ovenproof dish and stir in the saffron. Pour the hot stock over, then stir, cover, and leave to stand for 4–5 minutes. Stir in the sultanas, almonds and preserved lemon; season with salt and pepper. Dot half of the butter over the top and bake for 10 minutes until heated through.
3 In the meantime, toast the whole spices in a dry frying pan for 2 minutes or until fragrant. Using a pestle and mortar, grind them to a powder, then stir in the cinnamon, garlic and 2–3 tablespoons of the olive oil to make a thick, spreadable paste. Smear the mixture over the fish fillets.
4 Heat the remaining oil in a large, non-stick frying pan over a medium-high heat. Fry the fish for 4–5 minutes on each side until cooked and crisp.
5 Remove the couscous from the oven and stir in the remaining butter and coriander. Serve the fish with the couscous and a tomato and rocket salad.

PARMESAN-CRUSTED COD WITH BUTTERED SWEETCORN

Buttery puréed corn is absolutely delicious – it lifts ordinary frozen sweetcorn to new heights.

2 tbsp plain flour • 50g/1¾oz Parmesan cheese, grated • 2 tbsp finely snipped chives • 4 skinless cod fillets, each about 175g/6oz • 1 egg white, beaten • 4 tbsp olive oil • 450g/1lb fresh penne pasta • salt and freshly ground black pepper
BUTTERED SWEETCORN: 350g/12oz/heaped 2 cups frozen sweetcorn • 1 bay leaf • ¼ tsp caster sugar • 40g/1½oz butter

1 To make the buttered corn, put the sweetcorn in a saucepan with the bay leaf and add enough water just to cover. Bring to the boil, then turn the heat down and simmer for 3–4 minutes until soft.
2 In the meantime, mix the flour, Parmesan and chives together on a plate and season with a little salt and pepper; set aside.
3 Drain the sweetcorn and transfer to a blender, discarding the bay leaf. Add the sugar and blend to a fairly smooth purée. Return to the pan. Add half the butter and season to taste, then warm through.
4 Dip the fish into the egg white, then dust in the Parmesan mixture to coat. Heat the olive oil in a large, non-stick frying pan over a medium heat. Fry the fish for 4 minutes on each side or until cooked and golden.
5 At the same time, bring a saucepan of salted water to the boil and cook the penne for 2 minutes until al dente. Drain, then toss in the remaining butter. Serve the fish with the buttered sweetcorn and the penne.

SALMON IN LEMONY BUTTER SAUCE

This rich, lemony sauce makes a heavenly accompaniment to succulent salmon fillets, but it's another one of those adaptable sauces that marries well with white fish too.

450g/1lb new potatoes • 4 salmon fillets, each about 175g/6oz • 2 tbsp olive oil • juice of ½ lemon • 450g/1lb/3 cups frozen petit pois • salt and freshly ground black pepper
LEMONY BUTTER SAUCE: juice of 1 small lemon • 3 tbsp double cream • 200g/7oz butter, diced • 1 handful of parsley, leaves chopped

1 Preheat the oven to 200°C/400°F/Gas 6. Cook the potatoes in a saucepan of boiling salted water for 15–20 minutes or until tender; drain.
2 In the meantime, season the salmon with salt and pepper. Heat the olive oil in a large, non-stick frying pan over a high heat. Fry the salmon for 2 minutes on each side, then transfer to a roasting tin. Squeeze the lemon juice over and roast for 6 minutes or until just cooked but still slightly opaque in the centre.
3 To make the sauce, put the lemon juice in a small pan, then add the cream and 2 tablespoons of water and set over a low heat. Add the butter, a little at a time, stirring well, until it has all been incorporated and the sauce is thick and creamy. Stir in the parsley and season to taste.
4 Cook the peas in boiling salted water for 3–4 minutes until tender, then drain. Serve the salmon with the sauce spooned over and the potatoes and peas on the side.

PEPPER-CRUSTED TUNA WITH BEAN COMPÔTE

Tuna has a meaty texture that works really well with this crunchy peppercorn coating. The sugar tempers the heat of the pepper a little, so don't be tempted to leave it out.

300g/10½oz/heaped 1½ cups couscous • 500ml/17fl oz/2 cups hot vegetable stock • 4 handfuls of trimmed fine green beans • 1 handful of cherry tomatoes, cut in half • 1 handful of pitted black olives • 2 garlic cloves, crushed • 135ml/4½fl oz/generous ½ cup olive oil • 2 tbsp balsamic vinegar • 4 tuna steaks, each about 200g/7oz • 2 tbsp coarsely ground black peppercorns • 1 tsp muscovado sugar

1 Put the couscous in a bowl and pour the hot stock over to cover. Stir, cover, and leave to stand for 5–6 minutes until the stock is absorbed. Fluff up the couscous with a fork, then set aside, covered.
2 In the meantime, blanch the beans in boiling salted water for 2 minutes. Drain and rinse under cold running water. Transfer to a saucepan and stir in the tomatoes, olives and garlic. Pour in 6 tablespoons of the olive oil and the balsamic vinegar, then warm over a low heat for 4–5 minutes.
3 In the meantime, brush the tuna steaks with a little of the remaining olive oil. Mix the ground peppercorns and sugar together and press firmly over both sides of the tuna to coat.
4 Heat the rest of the oil in a griddle pan over a medium-high heat. Griddle the tuna for about 2 minutes on each side until seared but still slightly pink in the centre (the exact cooking time will vary depending on the thickness of the steaks). Serve the tuna with the bean compôte and couscous.

BAKED SEA BASS IN NEWSPAPER PARCELS

Cooking fish in a newspaper or baking paper parcel keeps it moist and succulent, and much of the skin comes away as the fish is unwrapped. You will need four sheets of newspaper in total.

4 small whole, cleaned and descaled sea bass • 450g/1lb trimmed green beans
DRESSING: 125ml/4fl oz/½ cup extra virgin olive oil • 1 large, ripe tomato, deseeded and roughly chopped • 2 tbsp finely chopped fennel • 1 shallot, finely chopped • 1 garlic clove, crushed • finely grated zest and juice of 1 lime • 1 small dried chilli (optional) • salt and freshly ground black pepper

TO SERVE: crusty bread

1 Preheat the oven to 220°C/450°F/Gas 7.
2 Carefully dampen four sheets of newspaper and wrap one fish in each. (You can also use baking paper for this.) Place the parcels in a roasting tin and bake for 20 minutes or until the fish is cooked.
3 In the meantime, cook the green beans in boiling salted water for 4–5 minutes until tender; drain.
4 To make the dressing, pour the oil into a small saucepan. Stir in the tomato, fennel, shallot, garlic, lime zest and juice and crumble in the chilli, if using. Season with salt and pepper and heat gently over a low heat until warm. Pour the dressing into a jug.
5 Serve the fish, still wrapped in newspaper, so that diners can open the parcel at the table and help themselves to the dressing. Serve with the green beans and slices of crusty bread.

FISH KOFTAS WITH COCONUT RICE

Spicy, delicious and easy to make, these skewers of minced fish also make great barbecue food. You will need 8 metal skewers.

1 tbsp coriander seeds • 1 tbsp cumin seeds • 250g/9oz skinless white fish fillets • 250g/9oz peeled raw prawns • 1 tsp ground cinnamon • 1 tsp ground ginger • 1 garlic clove, peeled • finely grated zest of 1 lemon • 1 tsp brown sugar • 2 tbsp desiccated coconut • 2 tbsp olive oil • salt
COCONUT RICE: 250g/9oz/1¼ cups basmati rice • 400ml/14fl oz/generous 1½ cups tinned coconut milk

TO SERVE: mixed leaf salad

1 Put the rice in a medium-sized saucepan with the coconut milk and 200ml/7fl oz/scant 1 cup water. Bring to the boil, then turn the heat down, cover, and simmer for 15 minutes until the rice is cooked and the water absorbed. Remove from the heat and leave to stand, covered, until ready to serve.
2 While the rice is cooking, toast the whole spices in a dry frying pan for 2–3 minutes until fragrant. Using a pestle and mortar, grind them to a powder.
3 Put the fish and prawns in a food processor and add the ground spices and garlic. Blitz to a coarse paste, then spoon the mixture into a bowl. Stir in the lemon zest, sugar and coconut until combined. Season with salt. Form the mixture into eight sausage-shaped koftas around the skewers.
4 Heat the olive oil in a large, non-stick frying pan over a medium heat. Fry the koftas for 6–7 minutes, turning, until golden. Serve with the coconut rice and a mixed leaf salad.

LINGUINE WITH CLAMS & WHITE WINE

This is my version of spaghetti vongole – one of my absolute favourite classic Italian dishes. The recipe works beautifully with mussels, too.

400g/14oz dried linguine pasta • 2 tbsp olive oil
3 shallots, finely chopped • 2 garlic cloves, sliced
• 1kg/2lb 4oz clams, cleaned and rinsed well
• 100ml/3½fl oz/generous ⅓ cup dry white wine
• 1 handful of parsley, leaves chopped

TO SERVE: tomato and red basil salad

1 Bring a large saucepan of salted water to the boil and cook the linguine for 2 minutes less than instructed on the pack until almost al dente.
2 In the meantime, heat the olive oil in a large, deep frying pan over a medium-low heat. Fry the shallots and garlic for 2 minutes, then add the clams.
3 Turn the heat up, stir, and add the wine. Cover with a lid and cook for 5 minutes or until the clams have opened. Discard any that remain closed.
4 Drain the linguine and transfer to the pan with the clams. Cook over a low heat for 2 minutes, stirring occasionally. Stir in the parsley and serve with a tomato and red basil salad.

FIG, LENTIL & FETA SALAD

Fresh figs have a fantastic affinity with lentils and salty feta. Goat's cheese works very well too.

300g/10½oz/1½ cups Beluga or Puy lentils • 4 tbsp extra virgin olive oil • 1 onion, chopped • 1 garlic clove, crushed • 1 tsp finely chopped rosemary • 3 tbsp balsamic vinegar • 3 ripe figs, cut into small bite-sized pieces • 250g/9oz feta cheese, crumbled • salt and freshly ground black pepper

TO SERVE: rocket salad and crusty bread

1 Cook the lentils in boiling water for 20 minutes or until tender.
2 In the meantime, heat 2 tablespoons of the olive oil in a saucepan over a medium heat. Fry the onion, garlic and rosemary for 2 minutes until softened.
3 Drain the cooked lentils and add them to the pan with the onion. Stir in the balsamic vinegar and remaining oil. Season with salt and pepper.
4 Scatter the figs and feta over the lentils. Season with a little extra pepper and serve warm with a rocket salad and slices of crusty bread.

FETA & SWEETCORN FRITTERS WITH SALSA >

These tasty fritters always go down a storm, with the salsa adding a real lift.

350g/12oz/heaped 2 cups frozen sweetcorn, defrosted • 3 eggs, separated • 1 red onion, finely chopped • 2 tbsp chopped chives • 50g/1¾oz/ scant ½ cup self-raising flour • 150g/5½oz feta cheese, crumbled • 30g/1oz butter
SALSA: 1 avocado, pitted and diced • 1 mango, pitted and diced • 1 papaya, deseeded and diced • 1 red onion, chopped • 1 red pepper, deseeded and diced • juice of 1 lime • 1 handful of coriander, leaves chopped • salt and freshly ground black pepper

TO SERVE: lime wedges and rocket salad

1 Put the sweetcorn in a large bowl. Add the egg yolks, red onion and chives, then stir in the flour and feta. Season with salt and pepper.
2 Whisk the egg whites until they form stiff peaks and fold them gently but thoroughly into the sweetcorn mixture.
3 Melt a third of the butter in a large, non-stick frying pan over a medium heat. Place 4 generous tablespoons of the batter in the pan, leaving a little space between each one, and cook for 2–3 minutes on each side until golden. Keep the fritters warm and repeat, using the rest of the batter and butter, to make 12 fritters in total.
4 In the meantime, make the fruit salsa. Combine all the ingredients in a bowl and season to taste.
5 Serve three fritters per person with lime wedges, the fruit salsa and a rocket salad on the side.

SAVOURY CORN TARTLETS

15g/½oz butter, plus extra for greasing • 450g/1lb new potatoes • 225g/8oz ready-rolled puff pastry • 2 eggs • 3 tbsp mascarpone cheese • 4 tbsp grated Parmesan cheese • 150g/5½oz/1 cup frozen sweetcorn, defrosted • 1 tsp thyme leaves • 450g/ 1lb broccoli florets • salt and freshly ground black pepper

1 Preheat the oven to 220°C/425°F/Gas 7 and lightly grease a 12-cup bun tin.
2 Boil the potatoes in a pan of salted water for 15–20 minutes until tender; drain, then toss in the butter.
3 In the meantime, cut discs from the rolled out pastry and use to line the bun tin.
4 Beat the eggs and mascarpone in a large bowl until smooth, then stir in the Parmesan, sweetcorn, thyme and seasoning. Spoon the filling into the tart cases and bake for 8–10 minutes until cooked.
5 While the tarts are baking, steam the broccoli for 5 minutes until tender. Serve the tarts with the new potatoes and broccoli.

CHEESY SWEET POTATOES

This delicious, meat-free main meal is rich and warming for chilly winter nights. If you can't find Taleggio, try another good melting cheese, such as French Reblochon or the Irish Gubbeen.

1kg/2lb 4oz sweet potatoes, peeled and diced • 600ml/21fl oz/scant 2½ cups double cream • 2 garlic cloves, peeled • 2 tbsp thyme leaves • 200g/7oz Taleggio cheese, cut into bite-sized pieces • salt and freshly ground black pepper

TO SERVE: watercress, rocket and spinach salad

1 Cook the sweet potatoes in boiling, salted water for 10–15 minutes until tender.
2 In the meantime, preheat the grill to high.
3 Pour the cream into a heavy-based saucepan and add the garlic, thyme, a pinch of salt and a grinding of black pepper, then bring to the boil.
4 Drain the potatoes and spoon them into a large gratin dish or shallow ovenproof serving dish. Scatter the Taleggio over the potatoes and pour the cream mixture over to coat.
5 Season with a little extra pepper and grill for 3–4 minutes until bubbling and light golden. Serve with a watercress, rocket and spinach salad.

COURGETTE & SULTANA PENNE

You could also serve this simple pasta dish with a scattering of crisp, golden breadcrumbs (see page 80), if liked.

450g/1lb dried penne pasta • 2 tbsp plain flour • 2 courgettes, cut into matchsticks • 3 tbsp olive oil • 2 garlic cloves, sliced • ½ tsp fennel seeds • 2 handfuls of pine nuts • 150g/5½oz/scant 1¼ cups sultanas • finely grated zest of 1 lemon • salt and freshly ground black pepper

TO SERVE: green leaf salad

1 Bring a large saucepan of salted water to the boil and cook the penne for 2 minutes less than instructed on the pack until almost al dente.
2 In the meantime, season the flour with salt and pepper. Toss the courgettes in the seasoned flour until lightly dusted.
3 Heat the olive oil in a large, deep, non-stick frying pan over a medium heat. Fry the courgettes, garlic and fennel seeds for 1–2 minutes, stirring regularly, until the courgettes are light golden.
4 Stir in the pine nuts and sultanas, then cook, stirring, for a further 1 minute until the nuts are golden and the sultanas softened. Add the lemon zest and season to taste.
5 Using a slotted spoon, lift the pasta out of its cooking water and add to the frying pan. Cook for 2 minutes, stirring, until the pasta is al dente and absorbs the flavours of the other ingredients. Serve with a green leaf salad.

RICOTTA & FRESH HERB FRITTATA

This simple frittata is great for a swift dinner, served with olive ciabatta and a mixed leaf salad.

9 large eggs, lightly beaten • 30g/1oz butter • 250g/9oz ricotta cheese • 1 small bunch of spring onions, thinly sliced • 1 small bunch of chives, snipped • salt and freshly ground black pepper

TO SERVE: olive ciabatta bread and mixed leaf and tomato salad

1 Preheat the grill to high.
2 Season the eggs with salt and pepper. Melt the butter in a large, deep, non-stick frying pan with a heatproof handle. Pour in the eggs and cook over a low heat for 10 minutes until the base of the frittata is set and light golden.
3 Dollop small spoonfuls of the ricotta over the top, then place the frittata under the grill for 3–5 minutes or until the top is just set.
4 Scatter the spring onions and chives over the frittata, then serve cut into wedges with slices of ciabatta and a mixed leaf and tomato salad.

COURGETTE & CANNELLINI BEAN SOUP

This gorgeous, thick soup is delicious finished with a good drizzle of fruity extra virgin olive oil.

6 tbsp extra virgin olive oil • 1 small onion, chopped • 2 celery stalks, chopped • 2 garlic cloves, crushed • 2 handfuls of parsley, leaves chopped • 850g/1lb 14oz courgettes, roughly chopped • 400g/14oz tinned cannellini beans, drained and rinsed • salt and freshly ground black pepper

TO SERVE: crusty bread and blue cheese, such as Roquefort or Gorgonzola

1 Heat 2 tablespoons of the olive oil in a saucepan over a medium heat. Fry the onion, celery, garlic and half the parsley for 4–5 minutes until softened but not coloured.
2 Add the courgettes and fry for a further 5 minutes until softened and beginning to colour.
3 Stir in 125ml/4fl oz/½ cup water and the cannellini beans. Cook for 8–10 minutes, crushing the beans slightly with the back of a fork. Season with salt and plenty of pepper.
4 Spoon the soup into shallow bowls, drizzle with the remaining olive oil and sprinkle over the rest of the parsley. Serve with slices of crusty bread and a blue cheese of your choice.

CHERRY TOMATO CLAFOUTIS

This savoury dish is based on the well-known sweet dessert, and makes a great dinner served with a rocket salad.

15g/½oz butter • 4 tbsp grated Parmesan cheese • 300g/10½oz cherry tomatoes • 6 eggs, beaten • 250ml/9fl oz/1 cup double cream • 90g/3¼oz/ ¾ cup plain flour, sifted • 8 slices of ciabatta bread • extra virgin olive oil, for drizzling •a few basil leaves • salt and freshly ground black pepper

TO SERVE: rocket, spinach and watercress salad

1 Preheat the oven to 200°C/400°F/Gas 6.
2 Grease four individual gratin dishes or 1 large dish with butter. Scatter 1 tablespoon of the Parmesan over the bottom of the dishes, then arrange the tomatoes evenly on top. Set aside.
3 Beat the eggs, double cream and remaining Parmesan together until light and fluffy, then fold in the flour. Season with salt and pepper. Pour the mixture carefully over the tomatoes.Cook for 15–20 minutes until risen and golden.
4 In the meantime, heat a griddle pan over a high heat. Griddle the ciabatta in two batches, for 4–5 minutes, turning once, or until toasted and charred in places. Drizzle a little olive oil over each slice.
5 Scatter the basil over the clafoutis and serve warm with the ciabatta and a rocket, spinach and watercress salad.

→

THIRTY MINUTES GIVES ENOUGH TIME TO PREPARE SOME SERIOUSLY BEAUTIFUL FOOD – AND YET IT ACTUALLY ISN'T A HUGE CHUNK OUT OF THE DAY. IT GOES TO PROVE THAT FAST FOOD CAN BE FABULOUS HOME-COOKED FOOD. TRY ONE FORKFUL OF COURGETTE FLOWER RISOTTO OR LAMB KEBABS WITH JEWELLED COUSCOUS AND I'M SURE YOU'LL AGREE.

→

THIRTY-
MINUTE
MEALS

STICKY CHICKEN WITH ALMOND COUSCOUS

You could substitute pieces of chicken breast or thigh meat for the wings, if preferred.

12 small chicken wings • juice of 1 orange • 1 tbsp clear honey • 2 tsp mild curry paste • 300g/10½oz/ heaped 1½ cups couscous • 500ml/17fl oz/2 cups hot vegetable or chicken stock • 1 large handful of toasted flaked almonds • 1 large handful of sultanas • 90g/3¼oz butter • 1 handful of parsley, leaves chopped • salt and freshly ground black pepper

TO SERVE: mixed leaf and herb salad

1 Preheat the oven to 200°C/400°F/Gas 6.
2 Arrange the chicken wings in a roasting tin, then season with salt and pepper. Mix the orange juice, honey and curry paste together and spoon it over the chicken. Turn the chicken in the mixture until coated, then roast for 25 minutes until cooked through and golden.
3 In the meantime, put the couscous in a shallow ovenproof dish and pour the hot stock over to cover. Stir, cover, and leave to stand for 4–5 minutes until the stock is absorbed. Fluff up the couscous with a fork and stir in the almonds and sultanas, season with salt and pepper. Dot half of the butter over the top and bake for 10 minutes or until heated through.
4 Remove the couscous from the oven and stir in the remaining butter and parsley. Spoon into a serving dish and top with the chicken, pouring over any sticky juices left in the roasting tin. Serve with a mixed leaf and herb salad.

PROSCIUTTO-WRAPPED CHICKEN PARCELS

These succulent chicken parcels encase flavoursome sun-dried tomatoes and aromatic sage. It's best to use small sage leaves.

4 skinless, boneless chicken breasts, each about 175g/6oz • 8 sun-dried tomatoes in oil, drained • 8 small sage leaves • 8 slices of prosciutto • 2 tbsp olive oil • 5 tbsp dry white wine • 450g/1lb new potatoes • 30g/1oz butter • 450g/1lb/3 cups frozen peas • salt and freshly ground black pepper

1 Place a chicken breast between 2 sheets of clingfilm and flatten with a meat mallet or rolling pin; repeat with the remaining chicken. Halve each breast and season with salt and pepper.
2 Place a sun-dried tomato and a small sage leaf towards the end of each piece of chicken. Roll each piece three times, then wrap in a slice of prosciutto to make a parcel.
3 Heat the olive oil in a large, non-stick frying pan over a medium heat. Fry the parcels for 10 minutes on each side or until the prosciutto is golden and the chicken cooked through. Pour in the wine and season to taste. Cook, scraping any bits from the bottom of the pan, for a further 3 minutes until the wine has reduced.
4 In the meantime, cook the new potatoes in a saucepan of boiling salted water for 15–20 minutes until tender; drain and toss in half the butter.
5 Cook the peas in boiling water for 3–4 minutes. Drain and toss in the remaining butter. Serve the chicken with the peas and new potatoes.

BAKED CHICKEN BREASTS IN TOMATO & MASCARPONE

A handful of black olives added to the creamy tomato sauce will add an extra depth of flavour, and a lovely contrast in colour.

4 skinless, boneless chicken breasts, each about 175g/6oz • 3 shallots, chopped • 2 garlic cloves, sliced • 300g/10½oz cherry tomatoes, cut in half • 6 tbsp dry white wine • 2 tbsp olive oil • 4 tbsp mascarpone cheese • 1 small handful of basil leaves • salt and freshly ground black pepper

TO SERVE: spinach salad and ciabatta bread

1 Preheat the oven to 200°C/400°F/Gas 6.
2 Arrange the chicken breasts in an ovenproof dish and scatter the shallots and garlic over. Place the tomatoes on top of and around the chicken.
3 Pour in the wine, drizzle the olive oil over the chicken and season with salt and pepper. Bake for 20 minutes.
4 Remove from the oven and dot the mascarpone randomly over and around the chicken. Return the dish to the oven for a further 5 minutes until the mascarpone just starts to melt in little puddles. Scatter with basil leaves and serve with a spinach leaf salad and slices of ciabatta.

GOLDEN TURKEY STEAKS WITH TARATOR

Tarator sauce is a speciality of Turkey, where it is often served with grilled fish or chicken. It's great with turkey breasts, too. Try not to over-process the sauce – you don't want it to be too smooth.

3 tbsp plain flour • 1 tbsp finely chopped parsley leaves • 4 turkey steaks, each about 175g/6oz • 1 egg, beaten • 3 tbsp olive oil • 1.25kg/2lb 12oz tinned butter beans, drained and rinsed • 2 garlic cloves, crushed • 4 tbsp extra virgin olive oil
TARATOR: 2 small slices of day-old white bread, crusts removed • 2 garlic cloves, crushed • 75g/2½oz/heaped ½ cup walnut pieces • juice of ½ lemon, or to taste • 5 tbsp extra virgin olive oil • salt and freshly ground black pepper

TO SERVE: mixed leaf salad

1 To make the tarator sauce, put the bread in a food processor and process to coarse crumbs. Add the garlic and walnuts, then pulse to a coarse paste. Add the lemon juice and olive oil, season with salt and pepper, then blend briefly until combined. Set aside.
2 Mix the flour with the parsley and season to taste.
3 Dip the turkey briefly in the egg, shake to remove any excess, then dust in the flour mixture to coat.
4 Heat the olive oil in a large, non-stick frying pan over a medium heat. Fry the turkey for 4 minutes on each side or until golden and cooked through.
5 While the turkey is cooking, heat the butter beans, garlic and extra virgin olive oil in a pan until warmed through, stirring occasionally. Using a hand blender, purée the beans, then season. Serve the turkey with the puréed butter beans, tarator and a mixed leaf salad.

HONEYED DUCK IN POMEGRANATE SAUCE

450g/1lb new potatoes • 15g/½oz butter • 4 duck breasts, each about 175g/6oz • 2 tbsp clear honey • 3 tbsp extra virgin olive oil • 450g/1lb trimmed fine green beans • seeds from 1 pomegranate
POMEGRANATE SAUCE: 100ml/3½fl oz/generous ⅓ cup olive oil • 3 shallots, chopped • 2 garlic cloves, crushed • 1 handful of dried apricots, finely chopped • 2 tbsp pomegranate molasses • 1 tbsp clear honey • 4 tbsp Worcestershire sauce • 100ml/3½fl oz/generous ⅓ cup chicken stock • salt and freshly ground black pepper

1 Preheat the oven to 200°C/400°F/Gas 6.
2 Cook the new potatoes in a saucepan of boiling salted water for 15–20 minutes until tender; drain and toss in the butter.
3 In the meantime, make the pomegranate sauce. Heat half the olive oil in a pan over a medium heat. Fry the shallots and garlic for 2 minutes until softened. Add the apricots, molasses, honey and Worcestershire sauce. Stir in the stock and bring to the boil, then turn the heat down and simmer for 8–10 minutes until reduced and thickened; season.
4 Heat the remaining olive oil in a large, non-stick frying pan over a medium heat. Fry the duck breasts, skin-side down, for 2–3 minutes until the skin is golden, then turn over and cook for a further 2 minutes. Transfer the duck to a roasting tin and brush with honey. Season to taste and roast for 12 minutes until cooked.
5 Cook the beans in boiling salted water for 3–4 minutes until al dente; drain. To serve, slice the duck breasts and fan them out on plates. Spoon the sauce over, scatter pomegranate seeds on top, and serve with green beans and new potatoes.

CRISPY DUCK LASAGNE >

This isn't "lasagne" in the Italian sense, but layers of crisp wonton wrappers filled with a gorgeous, vibrant duck salad.

groundnut or sunflower oil, for deep frying • 8 wonton wrappers • 1 garlic clove, crushed • 1 tbsp clear honey • 1 tbsp light soy sauce • 1 tbsp tamarind paste • 1 tsp wholegrain mustard • juice of 1 lime • 500g/1lb 2oz skinless duck breasts, cut into strips • 1 large carrot, cut into ribbons • 4 spring onions, diagonally sliced • 1 small red pepper, deseeded and sliced • 1 handful of sugar snap peas • 1 handful of beansprouts • 2 handfuls of herb salad, to include coriander leaves • 2 tsp toasted sesame seeds • salt and freshly ground black pepper
DRESSING: 4 pieces of preserved stem ginger, chopped • 4 tbsp preserved stem ginger syrup • 2 tbsp light soy sauce • 4 tbsp groundnut oil

1 Preheat the grill to high.
2 Heat enough oil in a wok to deep-fry the wonton. Fry the wonton in 2 batches for a few seconds until golden, then drain on kitchen paper and set aside.
3 In a large bowl, mix together the garlic, honey, soy sauce, tamarind, mustard and lime juice. Toss the duck strips in the mixture and stir to coat. Grill the duck for 8–10 minutes, turning once and basting with the marinade, until glossy and cooked.
4 In the meantime, put all the vegetables and herb salad in a bowl. Mix together the ingredients for the dressing, season with salt and pepper, then spoon enough over the salad to coat it lightly.
5 Lay a wonton wrapper on each serving plate. Top with a good handful of the salad, then the duck. Place a second wonton wrapper on top of the duck. Drizzle with any remaining salad dressing, scatter with sesame seeds and serve at once.

< PORK BURGERS WITH BLUE CHEESE & RED ONION SALSA

These succulent burgers are best made from good-quality, finely minced pork. For the best flavour, choose a punchy blue cheese.

450g/1lb good-quality pork mince • 1 onion, finely chopped • 2 tbsp soy sauce • 115g/4oz blue cheese, such as Roquefort, Gorgonzola or Stilton, sliced • salt and freshly ground black pepper
RED ONION SALSA: 2 tbsp olive oil • 2 red onions, cut into thin wedges • 2 tbsp balsamic vinegar • 1 tbsp chilli oil

TO SERVE: 4 crusty bread rolls and rocket salad

1 Preheat the grill to high.
2 In a large bowl, mix together the pork mince, onion and soy sauce, then season with salt and pepper. Form the mixture into four burgers.
3 Grill the burgers for 4 minutes on each side until cooked through. Top each burger with a quarter of the cheese and grill until melted.
4 In the meantime, make the red onion salsa. Heat 1 tablespoon of the olive oil in a griddle pan over a high heat. Griddle the onion wedges for 10 minutes, turning occasionally, until softened and charred in places. Remove from the heat and stir in the balsamic vinegar, chilli oil and the remaining olive oil.
5 Place one half of a roll on each serving plate. Top with a burger and a spoonful of the onion salsa. Place the other half of the rolls to the side and serve with a rocket salad.

PORK IN MUSHROOM & MUSTARD SAUCE

This luxurious recipe makes a delicious dinner for a special occasion.

2 tbsp olive oil • 4 garlic cloves (2 sliced and 2 crushed) • 4 thick pork chops, each about 175g/6oz • 450g/1lb brown cap mushrooms, sliced • 6 tbsp Marsala • 4 tbsp double cream • 1 tbsp wholegrain mustard • 1 handful of parsley, leaves chopped • 90ml/3fl oz/generous ⅓ cup extra virgin olive oil • 600g/1lb 5oz courgettes, sliced • 1.25kg/2lb 12oz tinned haricot beans, drained and rinsed • salt and freshly ground black pepper

1 Heat the olive oil in a large, non-stick sauté pan over a medium heat. Fry the sliced garlic for 30 seconds, then add the chops. Cook for 6–8 minutes, turning once, until golden. Add the mushrooms to the pan and cook, stirring often, for a further 5 minutes.
2 Add the Marsala and cook for 3 minutes until reduced, then stir in the cream, mustard and parsley. Season with salt and pepper. Cook for a further 3 minutes or until the sauce has thickened and the chops are cooked through.
3 While the pork is cooking, heat 3 tablespoons of the extra virgin olive oil in a large, non-stick frying pan over a medium-high heat. Fry the courgettes for 3–4 minutes until golden.
4 Put the haricot beans in a pan with the remaining extra virgin olive oil and crushed garlic. Heat until warmed through, stirring occasionally. Using a hand blender, purée the beans, then season. Serve the pork and sauce with the bean purée and courgettes on the side.

CANNELLINI BEAN & SAUSAGE STEW

Use good-quality sausages with a high meat content and the results will be delicious. For fans of all things fiery, a crumbled dried chilli adds extra oomph, but you can leave it out, if preferred.

2 tbsp olive oil • 1 onion, sliced • 8 good-quality pork sausages • 400g/14oz tinned cherry tomatoes • 200ml/7fl oz/scant 1 cup beef or chicken stock • 1 tsp fennel seeds • 1 dried chilli (optional) • 400g/14oz tinned cannellini beans, drained and rinsed • 350g/12oz baby spinach leaves • 1 handful of parsley, leaves chopped • salt and freshly ground black pepper

1 Heat the olive oil in a casserole dish over a medium heat. Fry the onion and sausages for 5 minutes, stirring often, until the sausages are golden all over.
2 Add the tomatoes, stock and fennel seeds, then crumble in the chilli, if using. Add the cannellini beans, then season with salt and pepper.
3 Bring to the boil, then turn the heat down and simmer for 15 minutes. Stir in the spinach and cook for a further 5 minutes until the sausages are cooked and the sauce has reduced and thickened. Stir in the parsley and serve.

GAMMON WITH LENTILS & POACHED EGGS

Vincotto is a lovely, rich speciality vinegar from Italy, and its deep, sweet flavour marries beautifully with the earthiness of the lentils. Add salty gammon and a runny egg and you have a heavenly dish.

300g/10½oz/1½ cups Puy lentils • 4 gammon steaks, each about 175g/6oz • 5 tbsp extra virgin olive oil • a splash of white wine vinegar • 4 large eggs • 1 onion, chopped • 1 garlic clove, crushed • 2 tbsp vincotto or balsamic vinegar • salt and freshly ground black pepper

TO SERVE: rocket salad

1 Cook the lentils in boiling water for 20–25 minutes until tender.
2 In the meantime, preheat the grill to medium-high. Brush the gammon with 1 tablespoon of the olive oil and grill for 2–3 minutes on each side until cooked.
3 Bring a large frying pan of water to the boil and add the wine vinegar. Turn the heat down to low. Break the eggs, one at a time, onto a saucer, then slide them into the water. Quickly gather the whites neatly around the yolk using a spoon and poach for 3 minutes until cooked, but the yolk is still runny.
4 While the eggs are poaching, heat 2 tablespoons of the olive oil in a large, non-stick frying pan over a medium heat. Fry the onion and garlic for 2 minutes until softened. Drain the lentils, add them to the onions, then stir in the vincotto and the remaining olive oil. Season to taste.
5 Serve the lentils with the egg, gammon steaks and a rocket salad.

LAMB KEBABS WITH JEWELLED COUSCOUS

These lamb kebabs are inspired by a dish known as *arrosticini*, which is a speciality of the Abruzzo region in Italy. In Abruzzo, it is made with mutton, but lamb is just as delicious. You will need 4 metal skewers.

450g/1lb lamb fillet, fat trimmed, and diced • 300g/10½oz/heaped 1½ cups couscous • 500ml/ 17fl oz/2 cups hot vegetable or chicken stock • seeds from 1 pomegranate • 1 large handful of shelled, unsalted pistachio nuts • 4 tbsp frozen sweetcorn, defrosted • 1 handful of dried cranberries or sour cherries • 90g/3¼oz butter • 1 handful of coriander, leaves chopped • salt and freshly ground black pepper

TO SERVE: watercress salad

1 Preheat the oven to 200°C/400°F/Gas 6.
2 Thread 6 pieces of lamb onto each skewer.
3 Put the couscous in a shallow, ovenproof dish and pour the hot stock over to cover. Stir, cover, and leave to stand for 4–5 minutes until the stock is absorbed. Fluff up the couscous with a fork, then stir in the pomegranate seeds, pistachios, sweetcorn and cranberries.
4 Dot half of the butter evenly over the top and place in the oven for 10 minutes or until heated through. Remove from the oven and stir in the remaining butter and coriander. Keep warm.
5 Heat the grill to high. Season the lamb with salt and pepper, then grill for 5 minutes, turning often, until cooked through. Serve the lamb kebabs with the couscous and a watercress salad.

SEARED LAMB WITH CINNAMON ONIONS

Don't be tempted to add more cinnamon – you just want to give a pleasant hint of spice, rather than it being overwhelming.

450g/1lb lamb fillet, trimmed of any fat and sliced • 2 tbsp olive oil • 1 tsp thyme leaves • 1.25kg/2lb 12oz tinned chickpeas, drained and rinsed • 2 garlic cloves, crushed • 3 tbsp extra virgin olive oil • salt and freshly ground black pepper
CINNAMON ONIONS: 2 tbsp olive oil • 3 red onions, thinly sliced • 1 tsp ground cinnamon • 1 tbsp caster sugar • 100ml/3½fl oz/generous ⅓ cup red wine • 2 tbsp red wine vinegar

TO SERVE: spinach salad

1 To make the cinnamon onions, heat the oil in a large, non-stick frying pan over a medium heat. Fry the onions and cinnamon for 1 minute, stirring frequently. Add the sugar and cook for a further 1 minute. Pour in the red wine, wine vinegar and 3 tablespoons water. Bring to the boil, then turn the heat down and simmer for 20 minutes, stirring regularly, until the onions are soft and sticky.
2 In the meantime, brush the lamb with the olive oil, season with salt and pepper, then sprinkle with the thyme. Heat a griddle pan over a medium-high heat and sear the lamb for 2 minutes on each side for medium-rare, or until cooked to your liking.
3 Put the chickpeas in a pan with 3 tablespoons hot water, the garlic and extra virgin olive oil. Heat until warmed through, stirring occasionally. Using a hand blender, purée the beans, then season. Serve the lamb with the bean purée, the cinnamon onions and a spinach salad.

STEAK IN MARSALA

Marsala is a Sicilian fortified wine that adds a wonderful flavour to both sweet and savoury sauces. You don't have to pay a fortune for a bottle, and a little goes a long way, so it's well worth keeping some on hand.

600g/1lb 5oz floury potatoes, peeled and cut into chunks • 3 tbsp hot milk • 4 tbsp olive oil • 2 onions, very thinly sliced • 4 fillet steaks, each about 175g/6oz • 175ml/6fl oz/¾ cup Marsala • 450g/1lb broccoli florets • salt and freshly ground black pepper

1 Cook the potatoes in boiling salted water for 15–20 minutes until soft, then drain. Add the hot milk and 1 tablespoon of the olive oil, then mash until smooth. Keep warm.
2 In the meantime, heat 2 tablespoons of the olive oil in a large, non-stick frying pan over a medium heat. Fry the onions for 10 minutes, stirring regularly, until softened and golden in places.
3 Heat a large griddle pan over a high heat. Brush the steaks with the remaining oil, season with salt and pepper, then griddle for 2–3 minutes on each side for medium-rare.
4 Add the cooked onions to the pan with the steaks and stir in the Marsala. Bubble for 2–3 minutes until the Marsala has reduced and thickened and the onions are glossy.
5 While the steaks are cooking, boil the broccoli in salted water for 4–5 minutes until tender; drain. Serve the steaks with the sauce spooned over, and with the mashed potatoes and broccoli.

ROASTED MEATBALLS IN LEMON & BAY >

These tasty meatballs are simply roasted in white wine with wedges of lemon and fragrant bay leaves. Good-quality pork mince can be used instead of veal, if preferred.

450g/1lb minced veal • 100g/3½oz Parmesan cheese, grated • 1 tsp dried oregano • 6 sage leaves, finely chopped • 2 tbsp olive oil • 150ml/5fl oz/scant ⅔ cup dry white wine • 1 lemon, cut into thin wedges • 6 bay leaves • 450g/1lb dried spaghetti • salt and freshly ground black pepper

TO SERVE: green leaf salad

1 Preheat the oven to 220°C/425°F/Gas 7.
2 Put the mince into a bowl and stir in the Parmesan and herbs. Season with salt and pepper, then form into balls, each about the size of a small walnut.
3 Heat the olive oil in a large, non-stick frying pan over a high heat. Fry the meatballs for 3–4 minutes, turning occasionally, until lightly browned.
4 Transfer the meatballs to an ovenproof dish and pour in the wine. Scatter the lemon wedges and bay leaves over the top, then bake for 20 minutes until the meatballs are cooked through.
5 In the meantime, cook the spaghetti. Bring a large pan of salted water to the boil and cook the pasta for 10 minutes or until al dente; drain and toss with the meatballs and any juices. Transfer to a serving dish and serve with a green leaf salad on the side.

< SMOKED HADDOCK GRATIN

Instead of potatoes and spinach, crusty bread and a simple salad would also be good with this creamy fish gratin.

450g/1lb baby new potatoes • 55g/2oz butter • 1kg/2lb 4oz smoked haddock fillet • 1 bay leaf • 300ml/10½fl oz/scant 1¼ cups milk • 2 tbsp plain flour • 150ml/5fl oz/scant ⅔ cup double cream • 2 tsp wholegrain mustard • 2 egg yolks • 4 tbsp grated Parmesan cheese • 1kg/2lb 4oz spinach leaves, washed • freshly ground black pepper

1 Preheat the oven to 200°C/400°F/Gas 6.
2 Cook the new potatoes in boiling salted water for 15 minutes or until tender. Drain, toss in 1 tablespoon of the butter and keep warm.
3 In the meantime, place the haddock in a large frying pan, then add the bay leaf and pour in the milk. Cook for 5 minutes over a medium-low heat until the fish is just opaque. Remove from the pan. Check for any bones, then remove the skin and flake into large pieces. Transfer the haddock to an ovenproof dish. Strain the milk and reserve.
4 Melt 2 tablespoons of the butter in a saucepan over a medium heat. Add the flour and cook, stirring continuously, for 3 minutes. Gradually, pour in the poaching milk and cook, stirring, for 2 minutes or until thickened. Whisk in the cream, mustard and egg yolks, then season with pepper. Stir in half the Parmesan and spoon the sauce over the fish. Sprinkle the remaining Parmesan over the top and bake for 10 minutes until golden.
5 At the same time, cook the spinach in a pan for 2–3 minutes until wilted. Drain and toss in the remaining butter. Serve the gratin with the new potatoes and spinach.

MINI SALMON EN CROÛTES

Individual salmon and filo parcels with a watercress sauce… bliss!

450g/1lb skinless salmon fillet, cut into 1cm/½in cubes • 1 tsp lemon juice • 3 pieces preserved stem ginger, finely chopped • 2 tbsp currants • 90g/3¼ oz butter, melted • 1 tbsp chopped coriander leaves • 8 x 20cm/8in squares of filo pastry • 300ml/10½fl oz/scant 1¼ cups single cream • 1 large handful of watercress • 1 tbsp wholegrain mustard • 800g/1lb 12oz tinned flageolet beans, drained and rinsed • 2 tbsp extra virgin olive oil • 1 small handful of chopped parsley • salt and freshly ground black pepper

1 Preheat the oven to 200°C/400°F/Gas 6.
2 Put the salmon in a bowl. Stir in the lemon juice, ginger, currants, coriander and 4 tablespoons of the melted butter. Season with salt and pepper.
3 Lay one of the pastry squares on a clean work surface and brush lightly with some of the remaining melted butter. Top with a second sheet. Spoon a quarter of the salmon mixture in the centre of the top sheet and fold over the edges to create a square parcel and enclose the filling. Repeat to make 3 more parcels.
4 Transfer the parcels to a non-stick baking sheet, seam-side down, and brush with butter. Bake for 10 minutes or until the pastry is golden.
5 In the meantime, blend the cream and watercress in a food processor until smooth. Add the mustard and season to taste.
6 Put the beans in a pan with the olive oil. Heat until warmed through, stirring occasionally, then stir in the parsley. Serve the salmon parcels with the beans and the watercress sauce alongside.

CRAB & CORN CAKES WITH MANGO SALSA

This mango salsa is one of those recipes that you can play around with to suit your own palate and what's available – a little fresh chilli works well.

200g/7oz/1⅓ cups frozen sweetcorn, defrosted • 1 tbsp plain flour • 1 egg, beaten • 300g/10½oz white crabmeat • 1 small handful of parsley, leaves chopped • 3–4 tbsp olive oil • sunflower oil, for deep frying • 12 wonton wrappers
MANGO SALSA: 1 small red onion, finely chopped • 1 red and 1 yellow pepper, deseeded and diced • 1 ripe but firm avocado, pitted and diced • 1 ripe but firm mango, pitted and diced • 4 tomatoes, deseeded and diced • juice and finely grated zest of 2 limes • 1 large handful of coriander, leaves chopped • salt and freshly ground black pepper

1 To make the salsa, mix together all the ingredients in a bowl. Season with salt and pepper; set aside.
2 To make the crab cakes, put the sweetcorn, flour and egg in a bowl and stir until well mixed. Lightly fold in the crabmeat and parsley, then season.
3 Heat the olive oil in a large, non-stick frying pan over a medium heat. Place 4 generous tablespoons of the batter in the pan, leaving a little space between each one, and fry for 2–3 minutes on each side until golden. Drain on kitchen paper, keep warm, and repeat to make 12 fritters in total.
4 Heat enough sunflower oil in a wok or large pan to deep-fry the wontons. When the oil is very hot, fry the wontons for 30 seconds until golden and puffed up, then drain on kitchen paper. Serve straightaway with the fritters and salsa.

ROAST SEA BASS WITH STOVED POTATOES >

This works best with fillets cut from a large fish, but if you find that only small fish are available, allow two per person and use an extra roasting tin.

6 tbsp olive oil • 650g/1lb 7oz waxy potatoes, peeled and cut into small bite-sized pieces • 4 large garlic cloves, unpeeled • 4 large sea bass fillets • 2 lemons, cut into wedges • 250g/9oz mangetout • salt and freshly ground black pepper

1 Heat 4 tablespoons of the olive oil in a large, non-stick sauté pan over a high heat. Add the potatoes and garlic, stir to coat them in the oil, then turn down the heat to medium-low and cover with a lid. Cook for 20 minutes until soft and golden, giving the pan a shake from time to time to prevent sticking. Drain briefly on kitchen paper, season with salt, and keep warm.
2 In the meantime, preheat the oven to 200°C/400°F/Gas 6.
3 Lay the fish fillets in a roasting tin and pour the remaining olive oil over the top. Squeeze half of the lemon wedges over the fish and top with the remaining wedges. Season to taste, then roast for 10 minutes or until cooked.
4 Steam the mangetout for 3–4 minutes until tender. Serve the fish with the stoved potatoes, garlic and mangetout on the side.

< FISH TAGINE

Choose a selection of seafood, including fish, baby squid, langoustine, prawns, mussels and clams. Mussels are essential because of the gorgeous juices they release into the broth.

6 tbsp extra virgin olive oil • 1 red pepper, deseeded and finely chopped • a pinch of saffron • 2cm/¾in piece fresh ginger, peeled and grated • 600g/1lb 5oz very ripe tomatoes, deseeded and finely chopped • 150ml/5fl oz/scant ⅔ cup dry white wine • 1.5kg/3lb 5oz assorted raw shellfish and fish, cleaned and prepared as necessary • 1 small handful of parsley, leaves chopped • 300g/10½oz/heaped 1½ cups couscous • 500ml/17fl oz/2 cups hot vegetable stock • 30g/1oz butter • salt and freshly ground black pepper

TO SERVE: crusty bread and green salad

1 Heat the olive oil in a large, deep sauté pan over a low heat. Add the red pepper, saffron, ginger and tomatoes and cook gently for about 10 minutes, stirring occasionally, until the pepper and tomatoes are meltingly soft.
2 Pour in the wine, season with salt and pepper, then add the shellfish and any large fish. Cover with a lid and cook for 2 minutes.
3 Add the squid, if using, and any smaller fish at this point. Continue to cook for a further 5 minutes or until the fish is just cooked.
4 In the meantime, put the couscous in a bowl and pour the hot stock over to cover. Stir, cover, and leave to stand for 5–6 minutes until the stock is absorbed. Fluff up with a fork and stir in the butter.
5 Scatter the parsley over the tagine and serve with the couscous, bread for mopping up the juices, and a green salad.

TUNA FISHCAKES WITH TOMATO-CAPER SAUCE

The tomato-caper sauce is the perfect accompaniment for these simple fishcakes, but I have to confess, they're also fantastic with bottled ketchup!

500g/1lb 2oz tinned tuna in olive oil • 2 thick slices of white bread, crusts removed • 1 egg, lightly beaten • 150g/5½oz mature Cheddar cheese, grated • 4 tbsp olive oil • 300g/10½oz/2 cups frozen peas • salt and freshly ground black pepper
TOMATO-CAPER SAUCE: 3 tbsp olive oil • 1 onion, finely chopped • 2 garlic cloves, crushed • 400g/14oz tinned cherry tomatoes • 2 tsp caster sugar • 1 tbsp capers, drained and rinsed • 1 small handful of basil leaves, roughly torn

1 To make the sauce, heat the olive oil in a pan over a low heat. Fry the onion and garlic for 5 minutes until softened. Add the cherry tomatoes and sugar, then season with salt and pepper. Bring to the boil, then turn the heat down and simmer for 10–15 minutes until reduced and thickened. Add the capers and basil, then simmer for 5 minutes more.
2 In the meantime, put the tuna and its oil in a large bowl, then flake with a fork. Process the bread in a food processor to make fine crumbs, and add to the tuna. Stir in the egg and cheese, then season with salt and pepper. Form into eight fishcakes.
3 Heat the olive oil in a large, non-stick frying pan over a medium heat. Fry the fishcakes for 4–5 minutes, turning once, until golden. Drain the fishcakes on kitchen paper.
4 Cook the peas in boiling water for 3–4 minutes; drain. Serve the tuna fishcakes with the tomato-caper sauce and peas.

CRISPY BEAN CAKES WITH CHILLI-LIME DIP

This recipe makes the sort of quick and easy storecupboard meal that both vegetarians and meat eaters will enjoy.

800g/1lb 12oz tinned butter beans, drained and rinsed • 2 garlic cloves, crushed • 5 tbsp grated Parmesan cheese • 3 tbsp tomato ketchup • 100g/3½oz/1¼ cups fresh breadcrumbs • 3 tbsp olive oil • salt and freshly ground black pepper
CHILLI-LIME DIP: 6 tbsp chilli sauce • juice of 1 lime

TO SERVE: crusty bread and mixed leaf salad

1 To make the dip, mix the chilli sauce and lime juice together in a small bowl and set aside.
2 Put the butter beans in a large bowl with the garlic, Parmesan, ketchup and breadcrumbs. Using a hand blender, work to a coarser purée, or mash with a fork if you prefer the bean cakes to have a slightly coarser texture. Season with salt and pepper. Form into small, flat cakes about 3cm/1¼ in diameter.
3 Heat the olive oil in a large, non-stick frying pan over a medium heat. Fry the bean cakes for 2–3 minutes on each side until golden and crisp. (You will need to cook them in two batches.) Drain on kitchen paper and keep warm.
4 Serve the bean cakes with the chilli-lime dip, slices of crusty bread and a mixed leaf salad.

CREAMED MUSHROOMS WITH POLENTA

Any robust, meaty mushrooms will work well in this recipe. It's also good made with assorted wild mushrooms when they're in season.

3 tbsp olive oil • 4 shallots, finely chopped • 2 garlic cloves, crushed • 1kg/2lb 4 oz portobellini mushrooms, left whole • 100ml/3½fl oz/generous ⅓ cup Marsala • 200ml/7fl oz/scant 1 cup double cream • 2 tbsp wholegrain mustard • 1 small handful of tarragon, leaves finely chopped • 450g/1lb tenderstem broccoli • salt and freshly ground black pepper
POLENTA: 1 litre/35fl oz/4 cups vegetable stock • 250g/9oz/1⅔ cups instant polenta • 100g/3½oz Parmesan cheese, grated • 2 tsp coarsely cracked black peppercorns • 30g/1oz butter, softened

1 To make the polenta, bring the stock to a rolling boil in a pan. Add the polenta in a steady stream, stirring continuously with a large balloon whisk. Bring to the boil, then turn the heat down and simmer for 6–8 minutes until thickened.
2 Using a wooden spoon, stir in the Parmesan, pepper and butter. Taste and season with salt, if necessary, and keep warm.
3 Heat the olive oil in a large saucepan over a medium heat. Fry the shallots and garlic for 2 minutes or until softened. Add the mushrooms and cook for a further 2 minutes, stirring often. Pour in the Marsala and cook briefly until reduced. Turn the heat down a little, then stir in the cream, mustard and tarragon and warm through; season to taste.
4 In the meantime, steam the broccoli for 5 minutes until just tender. Serve the mushrooms on top of the polenta with the broccoli on the side.

TOMATO TARTE TATIN

For this summery tart, it's important to have a very hot oven to ensure the pastry is thoroughly cooked, puffed up and golden. I've suggested serving it with a rocket and Parmesan salad, and you could also scatter over a few toasted pine nuts, if liked.

450g/1lb new potatoes • 15g/½oz butter • 600g/1lb 5oz cherry tomatoes • 3 tbsp olive oil • ½ tsp caster sugar • 1 tbsp thyme leaves • 250g/9oz ready-rolled puff pastry • salt and freshly ground black pepper

TO SERVE: rocket and shaved Parmesan salad

1 Preheat the oven to 220°C/425°F/Gas 7.
2 Cook the new potatoes in boiling salted water for about 15–20 minutes or until soft. Drain and toss in the butter.
3 In the meantime, arrange the tomatoes, cut-side up, over the base of a 20cm/8in tarte tatin tin or round cake tin, about 4cm/1½in deep. Drizzle the tomatoes with the olive oil and sprinkle over the sugar and thyme, then season with salt and pepper. Bake for 5 minutes or until starting to soften.
4 Trim the pastry to fit the tin, leaving a 2cm/¾in overlap. Lay the pastry carefully over the tomatoes and tuck in the excess to make a border. Bake for 15 minutes or until the pastry is risen and golden.
5 Remove the tatin from the oven and carefully turn it out onto a plate. Serve warm with the new potatoes and a rocket and shaved Parmesan salad.

TOMATO, RICOTTA & SPINACH STRUDEL

The classic combination of ricotta and spinach is wonderful enclosed in crisp, light filo pastry.

2 tbsp olive oil • 1 garlic clove, crushed • 1 large onion, chopped • 500g/1lb 2oz tomatoes, cut in half and deseeded • 450g/1lb baby spinach leaves, washed • 250g/9oz ricotta cheese • 4 sheets of filo pastry, each about 25 x 30cm/10 x 12in • 40g/1½oz butter, melted • salt and freshly ground black pepper

TO SERVE: watercress salad

1 Preheat the oven to 220°C/425°F/Gas 7.
2 Heat the olive oil in a large saucepan over a medium heat. Fry the garlic and onion for 3 minutes until softened. Add the tomatoes and cook for 3 minutes until beginning to break down.
3 Put the spinach in a separate pan with only the water left clinging to the leaves after washing. Cook over a low heat for 2 minutes until wilted. Drain, squeeze out any excess moisture, then chop. Stir the spinach into the tomato mixture and add the ricotta. Season with salt and pepper and mix well.
4 Lay one sheet of filo pastry on a clean work surface and brush with a little of the melted butter. Top with a second sheet of pastry and brush with more butter. Repeat with the remaining filo, brushing each layer with butter. Spoon the spinach filling along the centre, then fold in the ends and the sides to form a rectangular-shaped parcel.
5 Carefully lift the parcel onto a non-stick baking sheet, seam-side down. Brush the parcel with the remaining butter and bake for 15 minutes until crisp and golden. Serve with a watercress salad.

PEA, ROSEMARY & MASCARPONE RISOTTO

Creamy risotto flecked with peas, rosemary and pools of mascarpone makes a totally irresistible dish. For non-vegetarians, some crisp pancetta crumbled over the top just before serving adds a nice touch.

3 tbsp olive oil • 1 onion, finely chopped • 1 tbsp chopped fresh rosemary • 225g/8oz/heaped 1 cup risotto rice • 300ml/10½fl oz/1¼ cups dry white wine • 750ml/26fl oz/3 cups hot vegetable stock • 55g/2oz Parmesan cheese, finely grated • 250g/9oz/scant 1½ cups frozen peas • 5 tbsp mascarpone cheese • salt and freshly ground black pepper

TO SERVE: spinach, rocket and watercress salad

1 Heat the olive oil in a large, deep sauté pan over a low heat. Fry the onion and rosemary for 2–3 minutes until the onion has softened, but not coloured. Add the rice and stir for 2–3 minutes until it is coated in the oil and glossy. Stir in the wine and bubble for 30 seconds.
2 Keep the vegetable stock hot over a low heat. Add a ladleful of stock to the rice and cook over a medium-low heat for 2–3 minutes, stirring continuously, until absorbed. Continue adding the stock, a little at a time, until it has been absorbed and the rice is soft, but still has a little resistance. This will take about 20–25 minutes. About 5 minutes before the rice is ready, stir in the peas and cook until heated through.
3 Add the Parmesan, then season with salt and pepper. Lightly fold in the mascarpone. Serve with a spinach, watercress and rocket salad.

COURGETTE FLOWER RISOTTO >

It's such a pity that courgette flowers make such a fleeting appearance in markets and shops because they're gorgeous fried in a crisp light batter, or stirred into a creamy risotto like this one. Take care with the saffron, since too much will mask the delicate flavour of the flowers.

3 tbsp olive oil • 1 onion, finely chopped • a pinch of saffron • 225g/8oz/heaped 1 cup risotto rice • 300ml/10½fl oz/1¼ cups dry white wine • 750ml/26fl oz/3 cups hot vegetable stock • 55g/2oz Parmesan cheese, finely grated • 5 tbsp mascarpone cheese • 2 handfuls of courgette flowers • salt and freshly ground black pepper

TO SERVE: courgette, herb and courgette flower salad

1 Heat the olive oil in a large, deep sauté pan over a low heat. Fry the onion and saffron for 2–3 minutes until the onion has softened, but not coloured. Add the rice and stir for 2–3 minutes until it is coated in the oil and glossy. Stir in the wine and bubble for 30 seconds.
2 Keep the vegetable stock hot over a low heat. Add a ladleful of stock to the rice and cook over a medium-low heat for 2–3 minutes, stirring continuously, until absorbed. Continue adding the stock, a little at a time, until it has been absorbed and the rice is soft, but still has a little resistance. This will take about 20–25 minutes.
3 Stir in the Parmesan, then season with salt and pepper. Lightly fold in the courgette flowers and the mascarpone. Serve with a courgette, herb and courgette flower salad.

VEGETABLE CURRY WITH COCONUT RICE

Poppadoms and mango chutney can also be served alongside the curry and basmati rice.

2 tbsp olive oil • 1 onion, chopped • 2 garlic cloves, chopped • 1 tbsp curry paste • 2 carrots, chopped • 2 parsnips, chopped • 2 potatoes, peeled and cut into bite-sized chunks • 2 courgettes, chopped • 1 handful of small cauliflower florets • 300ml/10½fl oz/scant 1¼ cups vegetable stock • 250g/9oz/1¼ cups basmati rice• 400ml/14fl oz/generous 1½ cups tinned coconut milk• 1 handful of sultanas • 2 tbsp mango chutney • 1 handful of toasted flaked almonds • salt and freshly ground black pepper

1 Heat the olive oil in a large saucepan over a medium heat. Fry the onion and garlic for 2 minutes, then stir in the curry paste. Add the vegetables and pour in the stock. Bring to the boil, then turn the heat down, cover, and simmer for 15-20 minutes or until the vegetables are tender.
2 In the meantime, put the rice in a medium-sized saucepan with the coconut milk and 200ml/7fl oz/scant 1 cup water. Bring to the boil, then turn the heat down, cover, and simmer for 15 minutes until the rice is cooked and the water absorbed. Leave to stand, covered, until ready to serve.
3 Strain the vegetables, saving the stock. Return two-thirds of the vegetables to the pan. Using a hand blender, purée the remaining vegetables, adding enough of the stock to make a sauce.
4 Gently stir the vegetable purée, sultanas and mango chutney into the curry. Season with salt and pepper, then reheat gently. Serve the curry with the almonds scattered over and the rice.

CURRIED PARSNIP SOUP

Hand blenders are fabulous tools for puréeing soups, and, of course, they are much easier to clean than a food processor or large blender. Adjust the amount of curry paste in this soup to suit your palate.

4 tbsp olive oil • 1 onion, chopped • 2 tsp mild curry paste, or to taste • 680g/1lb 8oz parsnips, cut into chunks • 1.2 litres/40fl oz/4¾ cups vegetable stock • 400g/14oz tinned chickpeas, drained and rinsed • 150ml/5fl oz/scant ⅔ cup double cream • 1 handful of parsley, chopped • salt and freshly ground black pepper

TO SERVE: crusty bread and goat's cheese

1 Heat 3 tablespoons of the olive oil in a large saucepan over a medium heat. Fry the onion for 2–3 minutes until softened. Stir in the curry paste, then add the parsnips and cook for a further 2–3 minutes.
2 Pour in the stock. Bring to the boil, then turn the heat down and simmer for 20 minutes or until the parsnips are tender.
3 In the meantime, heat the remaining olive oil in a large, non-stick frying pan over a medium heat. Fry the chickpeas, tossing the pan occasionally, for 8–10 minutes until golden and slightly crisp. Set aside until ready to serve.
4 Using a hand blender, purée the soup until smooth. Stir in the cream and parsley, season with salt and pepper and warm through. To serve, scatter the chickpeas over each bowl of soup, and accompany with slices of crusty bread and goat's cheese.

SPICY RED LENTILS

Coconut cream adds a really rich creaminess to this simple lentil dish. You can also use dried coconut milk powder but make it up slightly thicker than suggested on the packet – it should be the same consistency as coconut cream.

1 tbsp cumin seeds • 1 tbsp coriander seeds • 2 tsp ground ginger • 2 tbsp olive oil • 1 onion, chopped • 2 carrots, chopped • 1 small sweet potato, peeled and chopped • 400g/14oz/1⅔ cups dried red lentils • 400g/14oz tinned cherry tomatoes, drained • 900ml/31fl oz/3¾ cups vegetable stock • 1 tsp soft dark brown sugar • 5 tbsp coconut cream • 1 handful of parsley, leaves chopped • salt and freshly ground black pepper

TO SERVE: naan breads

1 Put the spices in a dry large saucepan and toast over a medium heat for 1–2 minutes, stirring, until they smell fragrant.
2 Pour in the olive oil and add the onion. Fry for 2 minutes, stirring, until slightly softened, then add the carrots, sweet potato, red lentils and cherry tomatoes.
3 Pour in the stock, add the sugar and season with salt and pepper. Bring to the boil, then turn the heat down and simmer for 20 minutes until the vegetables and lentils are tender.
4 Stir in the coconut cream and parsley, then cook for another 1 minute. Serve with naan breads.

POTATO, CHARD & GREEN BEAN BRAISE

Deliciously simple, this makes a great main course. Non-vegetarians could top it with a few slices of crisp pancetta, although it tastes very good as it is.

5 tbsp olive oil • 1 garlic clove, sliced • 1 onion, chopped • 800g/1lb 12oz potatoes, peeled and diced • 600g/1lb 5oz trimmed green beans, cut into 2.5cm/1in pieces • 1kg/2lb 4oz Swiss chard, trimmed and chopped • 8 slices of olive ciabatta bread • 150g/5½oz soft goat's cheese • salt and freshly ground black pepper

1 Heat 3 tablespoons of the olive oil in a large, deep, non-stick sauté pan over a medium heat. Fry the garlic and onion for 2 minutes, then add the potatoes, green beans, chard and 125ml/4fl oz/½ cup water. Season with salt and pepper.
2 Bring to the boil, then turn the heat down, cover, and simmer for 20 minutes until the vegetables are soft and the water is absorbed.
3 In the meantime, preheat the grill to high. Grill the olive ciabatta until lightly toasted. Drizzle the remaining olive oil over the toast and top each slice with a spoonful of goat's cheese; season with pepper. Serve the goat's cheese toasts with the braised vegetables.

ARTICHOKE, PINE NUT & PARMESAN TART

Puff pastry makes a great tart case but takes an age to make from scratch. Luckily chilled and frozen puff pastry is widely available now, so it seems silly not to make use of it. Look for the good-quality butter version.

450g/1lb baby new potatoes • 30g/1oz butter • 250g/9oz ready-rolled puff pastry • 300g/10½oz bottled artichokes, drained well • 250ml/9fl oz mascarpone cheese • 4 eggs • 150g/5½oz Parmesan cheese, grated • 1 tbsp toasted pine nuts • salt and freshly ground black pepper

TO SERVE: mixed leaf salad

1 Preheat the oven to 220°C/425°F/Gas 7.
2 Put the potatoes in a saucepan and add enough water to half cover them. Season with a little salt, add the butter, and cover with a lid. Cook for 20–25 minutes over a medium heat until the potatoes are tender, stirring from time to time to prevent them sticking.
3 In the meantime, line a 23cm/9in non-stick tart tin with the puff pastry. Arrange the artichokes evenly over the base of the pastry. Beat the mascarpone and eggs together until smooth. Stir in the Parmesan and season with salt and pepper.
4 Pour the mixture into the tart case and scatter the pine nuts over the top. Bake for 20 minutes or until puffed up and golden. Serve the tart with the potatoes and a mixed leaf salad.

AUBERGINE, MOZZARELLA & TOMATO BAKE >

This is also delicious made with silken tofu instead of the mozzarella, which makes it a great dish for vegans or those with a dairy allergy.

2 small aubergines, each cut into 8 long slices • 6 tbsp olive oil • 8 tomatoes, deseeded and chopped • 1 dried chilli, crumbled • 250g/9oz mozzarella cheese, diced • 100g/3½oz/1 cup walnut halves, roughly chopped • 1 small handful of parsley, leaves chopped • salt and freshly ground black pepper

TO SERVE: ciabatta bread and watercress salad

1 Preheat the oven to 200°C/400°F/Gas 6.
2 Heat a griddle pan over a high heat. Brush the aubergine slices with two-thirds of the olive oil and griddle for 5 minutes, turning once, until charred in places. (You will need to do this in two batches.)
3 In the meantime, heat the remaining oil in a large, non-stick frying pan over a medium heat. Add the tomatoes and chilli, season with salt and pepper, then fry for 2–3 minutes until softened.
4 Lay half the aubergine slices in a roasting tray and spoon half the tomato mixture on top. Scatter over the mozzarella, then make a second layer of aubergine to create a "sandwich" effect.
5 Scatter the remaining tomato mixture, the walnuts and parsley over the top. Bake for 6–8 minutes until heated through and the mozzarella starts to melt. Serve with ciabatta and a watercress salad.

INDEX